THE NOTICED
UN
ENTREPRENEUR

T0274599

THE UNNOTICED
ENTREPRENEUR

HOW ENTREPRENEURS CAN LEVERAGE THEIR AUTHENTICITY TO BUILD BRANDS

JIM JAMES

CAPSTONE
A Wiley Brand

Registered Office(s)
John Wiley & Sons, Inc., 111 River Street, Hoboken, NJ 07030, USA
John Wiley & Sons Ltd, The Atrium, Southern Gate, Chichester, West Sussex, PO19 8SQ, UK

For details of our global editorial offices, customer services, and more information about Wiley products visit us at www.wiley.com.

Wiley also publishes its books in a variety of electronic formats and by print-on-demand. Some content that appears in standard print versions of this book may not be available in other formats.

Library of Congress Cataloging-in-Publication Data Is Available:

ISBN 9781394195756 (Paperback)
ISBN 9780857089793 (ePDF)
ISBN 9780857089786 (ePub)
ISBN 9781907312731 (oBook)

Cover Design: Wiley
Cover Image: © Artishok/Shutterstock

Set in 11pt/15pt Minion Pro by Straive, Chennai, India.

SKY10086340_093024

This book is dedicated to my family.

To my steadfast wife, Erika, who has covered for me when I have been closed away in my office.

To my amazing daughters, Amity and Halo, who humoured me each morning on the school run as I shared my updates.

To Binkie, my beagle, who patiently waited for walkies.

Contents

Contents

Foreword by Brad Sugars

Without customers, you don't have a business; without a company, you'll have to work for someone else.

I knew from a young age that I wanted to be my own boss, make my own money, and have control over my life.

Having started ActionCOACH in Australia in 1993, we've grown the business coaching brand to have a presence in over 80 countries. We have thousands of coaches and franchise partners worldwide helping hundreds of thousands of business owners every day.

The hardest part for most of our clients is bringing in new revenue for their business.

I've been there, and I've successfully crossed the desert of no leads and no sales.

In the early years, before the internet and all the wonders of technology, I went on the road, hosting over 200 events a year. It was hard work, but I was in front of potential customers and constantly learned what they wanted.

I realised that I needed to get noticed more than I could by just doing in-person events. I collaborated with newspaper groups and radio stations, and in those first two years, a newspaper group in Australia put me in front of 288,000 business owners.

Partnerships are still a cornerstone of my brand-building strategy and should be a part of yours.

However, technology has also made being everywhere at once and personalization at scale simple, quick, cost-effective, and straightforward for even the least tech-savvy entrepreneur.

Technology is also making it possible to share experiences and learn from other entrepreneurs who solve the same mundane but essential marketing problems. From my studio in Las Vegas, I'm leveraging podcasting to share my messages about business growth, wealth, and leaving a lasting legacy.

When Jim interviewed me for The UnNoticed Entrepreneur podcast, he didn't ask me about what ActionCOACH does, but rather how I've built a global brand from scratch, without any outside investors. He wanted to know about my approach in the early days of "lumpy marketing" and the concepts in my latest book, *Raise your Hand Marketing*.

You see Jim's on a mission to discover and to share how entrepreneurs can build a brand without a big budget or expensive agencies to help.

I'm one of over 450 entrepreneurs who have shared their stories on his podcast and one of 50 selected for the third volume of the book series. He's uncorked his own bottle of "lumpy marketing" with me by sending me an almanack on Rum, which led to me writing this Foreword.

So, if this isn't a course, why am I recommending it to you? I'm a coach, after all!

Because we all need mentors to inspire us, coaches to instruct us, and peers to inform us.

This book is like having 50 private mastermind sessions with your peers. In the time it takes you to drink your morning coffee or afternoon tea, or have a nice glass of Rum, you'll learn how to solve a problem quickly and probably for free.

We both know that being an entrepreneur is not easy but learning from those who have gone before you becomes much easier than doing it alone.

Welcome to the unnoticed entrepreneur.

Brad Sugars
Founder
ActionCOACH
Las Vegas, NV
USA

Acknowledgements

Any author will tell you that their book is only possible due to the support and contribution of others.

In a way this is the most stressful part, because to leave anyone out would be the greatest mistake.

To my publishers at Capstone, a Wiley imprint, I am so grateful that you have taken an interest in *The UnNoticed Entrepreneur* series. To Annie Knight in the UK for first reaching out. To Susan Cerra in New York for ensuring that the books make it through production. To Alice Hadaway for her support on publicity, and Nick Mannion as he shepherds the books to stores. To the editors and proof checkers at Wiley – Premkumar Narayanan, Rathi Aravind, Aravind Kannankara, and their assistants who have tirelessly reviewed and corrected my mistakes – I am deeply grateful. Your efforts cover the cracks in my authorship.

To Brad Sugars, Founder of ActionCOACH, who agreed to contribute the Foreword. As an entrepreneur who has accomplished so much, I am grateful that he would be a guest on my podcast, invite me to be a guest on his show, and then also share his own thoughts on the importance of getting noticed at the front of this book.

To Jamie Smart, respected author and coach on the subject of clarity. A fellow Wiley author, Jamie kindly took my call on a

Sunday morning to talk through the importance of his area of expertise to entrepreneurs. I hope that I didn't ruin his vacation too much! I am grateful that he contributed a piece for readers on the direct connection between clarity, purpose, and business growth.

To the 50 entrepreneurs who have all shared their stories with me on the podcast. They no doubt thought that they had seen the last of me when we posted their episode. I hope that they find the chapters faithfully reflect our conversation and do them justice for the amazing entrepreneurs that they are.

To my father, Professor Louis James. My sage mentor. On one occasion, our call was interrupted by a magazine in Boston, requesting to write a multi-page article about his life work as a pioneering academic and scholar spanning Dickensian, Caribbean, and African literature. At the tender age of 90, he can still type more quickly than I ever would dream of and has the mental acuity that makes a dullard of AI.

To my sister, Dr. Shelley James. For rather annoyingly holding me to account, in a way that only siblings can. Without her, this book would have been much less work and much less of a work worth reading. We all need people who believe in us and ensure that we reach inside to be the best version of ourselves.

I want to thank you, the reader. An author's work is not complete until someone has purchased and engaged with the book. Your purchase validates the existence of this book. I interview entrepreneurs and curate their views for you. Having this book in your hands makes all my efforts worthwhile. I hope you find as much value in reading it as I have found in writing it.

And then to my family – Erika, Amity, and Halo. They have gone unnoticed too often as I have been away in the office trying to gather all the strands of this book together. Thanks to them for their patience and for being there with their smiles and laughter when I emerge from my study. You make all this worthwhile.

Introduction

Imagine,

If the iPhone had never been noticed, there would be no sleek touchscreens, no app revolution, and no seamless integration of phone, music, and internet in our pockets.

Imagine,

If Elon Musk's Tesla had remained just another ambitious project, it would never have gained the traction to disrupt the automotive industry with electric cars.

Imagine,

Just how dirty the world would be if James Dyson's bagless vacuum cleaners had gone unnoticed.

Imagine,

How many brilliant ideas are lost to obscurity simply because the founder needs to learn how to get the word out into the market.

Every day, countless innovations and solutions go undiscovered, not because they lack potential but because they never catch the public's eye.

Including possibly yours :(

Publicity isn't just about fame; it's about survival and success.

The need for recognition is as old as innovation itself. Take Thomas Edison, for example. His invention of the light bulb wasn't just a stroke of genius; it was a masterclass in publicity.

Edison didn't just invent the light bulb; he famously held a large public demonstration of his electric lighting system in 1879 at his Menlo Park, New Jersey laboratory.

In more recent history, Richard Branson's Virgin Group showcases the power of publicity. Through savvy media engagement and high-profile stunts, Branson turned Virgin from a small mail-order record retailer into a global conglomerate. His ability to capture the public's attention has been as crucial as his business acumen.

But what if these leaders hadn't mastered the art of getting noticed? Imagine if the iPhone launch had been a quiet affair, barely mentioned in the press. Would it have revolutionised the tech industry and our daily lives? What if Tesla's sleek, fast electric cars had remained a niche product for the eco-conscious elite, never gaining the widespread attention needed to transform the automotive landscape?

My question to you is, what will happen if you go unnoticed?

How will the world miss out?

Because you, and entrepreneurs like you, are the change makers that the world needs.

And because only some know how to get noticed for free, I've written this book. Inside are the stories of 50 entrepreneurs drawn from diverse industries and countries who have learnt how to build their brands to build a business. They all came onto my podcast and entrusted me with their stories, which I am privileged to share.

This book is my contribution to your effort to make that difference for good.

Approach

Inspired by Mason Currey's advice to Tim Ferris,[1] I've tried to retain the voices of my guests even through transcription and

---

[1] In *Tools of Titans*, Ferris said that Currey advised him to "get out of the way" and let the subject's words come through to the reader.

editing. My goal is for you to feel as though you are listening to them speaking to you directly. My role is as a facilitator, not a translator.

Quick Decisions

I created ten hashtags above each article to help you decide quickly if it interests you. These include, for example, #Entrepreneurship, #BrandBuilding, #MarketingStrategies, etc.

Quick Read

You can read an article in about 10 minutes. They can be read separately or in sequence.

Each chapter consists of two items:

- The Article: A conversation with the entrepreneur.
- Quick Response Code: Scan the code; the original podcast episode will play on your phone.

Common Themes

Reading these pages, you'll find themes that will resonate with your own experience as an entrepreneur:

- Clarity of Purpose: Knowing why you're in business and what you aim to achieve.
- Authenticity: Being genuine and transparent in your interactions.
- Building a Community: Engaging with people who support and amplify your vision.
- Getting in Front of People: Finding ways to make your presence known.
- Listening to Feedback: Valuing and acting on input from others.
- Sharing Knowledge Generously: Helping others grow and succeed.
- Personalisation at Scale: Making individualised connections with a broad audience.
- Leveraging Technology: Using tools and platforms to enhance your business.

Each entrepreneur's path to success is unique, reinforcing that there's no one-size-fits-all formula. Some seek the spotlight, while others avoid it, each finding their way to be noticed.

Take Aways

In the book's final section, I created a list of Ten Take Aways that could be used as a checklist in your own business. There is also a reference to a downloadable file with a comprehensive list of actionable insights, as including them in the printed book made this closer to an encyclopedia than an easy-to-read collection of essays.

Resources

At the end of the book, you will find:

- Key Take Aways: Ten of the recurring themes from all the interviews.
- Directory of Contributors: Contact information for the featured entrepreneurs.
- Tech Stack: Tools mentioned in the book.
- Bibliography: A list of recommended books and podcasts.

The Role of Artificial Intelligence

AI excelled at organising information and extracting insights, but without some human intervention, you would find that every interviewee "hails from a bustling hub of entrepreneurial activity . . . ".

Full disclosure: where the AI wrote copy that captures the essence of the transcript, I have used it instead of trying to rewrite it. I also wanted to keep a consistent format, even where it didn't exist during the interview, so I used AI to help me retain structure.

As much as I have tried to rectify the AI's errors, any errors and omissions are entirely my fault. Learning how to work with AI has been part of the experience of writing this book.

Finally, this is not just about "spin".

Publicity, or spin, is often associated with negative connotations. However, entrepreneurs and their companies need to be noticed to exist, and the same is true of individuals.

Recognition is a fundamental human need, rooted in the Greek concept of "Thymōs", or spiritedness. Francis Fukuyama's *The End of History and the Last Man* explores the concepts of "isothymia" (the need to be seen as equal) and "megalothymia" (the need to be seen as superior).

Of course, business is a competition; isothermic is not enough. To win, we have to attain megalothymia; to be seen as superior by the market.

This book will help you learn how your fellow entrepreneurs gained positions of superiority in their markets with affordable marketing strategies. You can use these in your business to impact the world.

Once you've done that, I welcome you as a guest on my podcast to tell your story.

Keep on communicating!

Jim A. James

The Importance of Clarity.

Jamie Smart
Clarity: The Entrepreneur's Compass

"If you don't know where you're going...
Any road will take you there..."
—George Harrison
Musician, film producer

"When do you get your best ideas?"

I've asked this question to thousands of people, from prison inmates to generals in the armed forces. I've asked countless business leaders, ranging from founders of entrepreneurial startups to corporate CEOs. In a survey of business people, the top three answers were as follows:

1. On vacation
2. In the shower
3. While travelling to and from work

The ideas that made a difference arrived at the times when they weren't even thinking about work. Almost everyone can relate to this and find their own examples of fresh, new thoughts arriving when the mind is in a more relaxed, contemplative state.

If a pond is clouded with mud, you cannot make the water clear. But when you allow the mud to settle, it will clear on its own because clarity is the water's natural state.

Clarity is your mind's natural state.

For many years, I've been sharing this simple metaphor in workshops and seminars with entrepreneurs, solopreneurs, and private individuals. As people allow their "mental mud" to settle, clarity emerges, and they discover that they have what they need for the job. This process empowers them, giving them a sense of direction and confidence in their decisions.

Every entrepreneur can recognise these "moments of clarity" as pivotal in the inspiration for their business. These moments, when harnessed, have the potential to transform not just businesses, but also lives. Yet, business owners often need to pay more attention to this innate capacity for clarity when they most need it.

And these days, we definitely need it.

As an entrepreneur, it's never been more critical to have clarity in realising, articulating, and sharing your purpose.

"Massive Transformational Purpose" (MTP) leads businesses to grow exponentially. Angel investor Salim Ismail details the DNA of growth companies in his book, *Exponential Organisations.*

- TED's MTP is to spread ideas
- Uber's MTP is to evolve the way the world moves
- Kickstarter's MTP is to help bring creative projects to life
- Duolingo's MTP is to give everyone access to education of the highest quality – for free
- LinkedIn's MTP is to create economic opportunity for every member of the global workforce
- Google's MTP is to organise the world's information and make it universally accessible and useful

So what is "purpose"?

Purpose is a thought; like all thoughts, it comes with a feeling. It may have some of these qualities…

- it may come with a feeling of gentle certainty or knowing…
- it may come as a sudden flash of realisation or a slow awakening…
- it may strike you as extremely obvious, with an "Of course! How did I not see this before?" quality…

You will have experienced this moment.

As an entrepreneur, you will have moved past this moment and taken action. You've summoned up the courage to turn your purpose into a business.

Now, it's time to get that business noticed.

It's your clarity of purpose that will attract people to your business. This truth applies to everyone: employees, partners, investors, and (of course) customers.

It will inspire passion, loyalty, and motivation in the people who share a common purpose with you.

Your authenticity, perseverance, and clarity of purpose will get you noticed.

Perhaps you weren't even thinking about work when you picked out this book.

Fifty fellow entrepreneurs are sharing their stories. I encourage you to take a moment after each chapter to go to the place where your best ideas come to you and allow the "mental mud" to settle.

Clarity will emerge.

You will discover that you have all that you need to decide where you're going, how to get there, and how to get noticed on purpose.

Yours in clarity.

Jamie Smart
London
England

Chapter One
Automate Authenticity.

Chris Larsen
*Founder and CEO Next Level Income, Asheville,
North Carolina, USA*

*"If you're working with 10 people,
100 people, or 1,000 people,
how do you remember special
occasions? How do you
ensure that you're impacting
someone's life in a way that is
important to them?"*

Helping Clients Make the Most of Their Money

#NextLevelIncome #FinancialServices #AutomatedAuthenticity
#ClientEngagement #InvestmentStrategy #RealEstateInvesting
#PersonalizedService #FinancialIndependence
#CustomerRelationshipManagement #InboundMarketing

Introduction

In the serene town of Asheville, North Carolina, Chris Larsen, the founder of Next Level Income, has crafted a unique approach to getting noticed in the crowded financial industry. His journey from a medical device sales engineer to a financial entrepreneur offers invaluable lessons for any business owner looking to elevate their brand and engage with their audience authentically.

The Genesis of Next Level Income

Chris Larsen's career began in the high-stakes environment of medical device sales, where he worked closely with surgeons to ensure optimal patient outcomes. This experience laid the foundation for his meticulous approach to business. "I spent 18 years in the medical device industry, working with surgeons, and the outcomes we sought were for patients. It was very important," he recalls. This background instilled in him the importance of precision and reliability, qualities he has carried over into his financial ventures.

Automating Authenticity

One of the most intriguing aspects of Larsen's strategy is his concept of "automating authenticity." In an industry where trust is paramount, maintaining genuine connections with clients can be challenging, especially as the business scales. Larsen explains, "If you're working with 10 people, 100 people, 1,000 people, how do you remember special occasions? How do you make sure that you're impacting someone's life in a way that is important to them?"

The answer lies in effective communication and systematisation. Larsen uses HubSpot, a customer relationship management tool, to keep track of client details and interactions. "I take notes. I use HubSpot, and I make sure that I have different things – who referred that person, are they married, do they have children, what is the why?" This meticulous record-keeping allows him to personalise his interactions, ensuring that each client feels valued and understood.

Building a Platform

For Larsen, the journey to financial independence is not just a personal goal but a mission to help others achieve the same. He emphasises the importance of building a platform to share valuable content. "You need to build a platform. Social media is a great, very inexpensive way to build a platform," he advises. Larsen leverages LinkedIn to connect with professionals and high-income earners, sharing daily content that ranges from articles to personal insights.

His approach to content is both generous and strategic. "Richard Wilson, who was the second guest on our podcast, said, 'Give away 80% of what you do and charge for 20%.'" By offering free resources like his book and podcast, Larsen attracts a wide audience, many of whom eventually become clients. "If you're listening, go to nextlevelincome.com. Click on the book link. You can download a free copy," he invites.

Engaging with Leads

Once potential clients are drawn in by the free content, Larsen has a well-defined process for engaging them further. "You need a way to engage people. A lot of people call this a lead magnet," he explains. His book serves as this magnet, leading to a series of follow-up emails and, eventually, a personal call. "You're going to get a daily email talking about what we do and inviting you to have a call with me at the end of that."

This method ensures that by the time Larsen speaks with a potential client, they are already familiar with his philosophy and approach. It also allows him to tailor his advice to their specific needs, making the interaction more meaningful and effective.

Personalisation at Scale

Maintaining authenticity while scaling a business is no small feat. Larsen's solution involves a combination of personal effort and strategic delegation. "At some point, you can't do it all. I can't have all the emails, all the conversations," he admits. To manage this, he employs an assistant who helps with follow-ups and reminders, ensuring that no client feels neglected.

Larsen also uses a variety of communication methods to reach his audience. "I send a physical mailing out as well. Some people say, 'Don't waste your time and money sending me that,' and other people say, 'Wow, I really like the fact that you do that.'" This multichannel approach allows him to meet clients where they are, whether they prefer digital communication or traditional mail.

Tailoring the Message

Understanding the diverse needs of his audience is crucial for Larsen. He has identified three primary avatars: young high-income professionals, middle-aged individuals with significant savings, and high-net-worth retirees. Each group has different needs and goals, and Larsen tailors his messaging accordingly.

"My messaging in my articles is always for all three of those avatars," he notes.

This tailored approach extends to his podcast, where he features guests from various backgrounds to appeal to his diverse audience. "We have young people on the podcast, 23-year-olds, and we have 70-some-year-old men on the podcast and everything in between," he says. By showcasing a range of perspectives, Larsen ensures that his content resonates with a broad spectrum of listeners.

The Role of the Podcast

Larsen's podcast serves as a cornerstone of his content strategy, providing a platform to share insights on making, keeping, and growing money. "The podcast is there to curate content for people that are learning ways to achieve financial independence," he explains. Topics range from tax strategies to investment opportunities, offering something for everyone interested in financial growth.

In addition to hosting his own podcast, Larsen appears as a guest on other shows to reach new audiences. "My goal is to produce a hundred podcasts a year, either of my own or other people's," he shares. This cross-pollination not only expands his reach but also allows him to learn from other experts in the field.

Conclusion

Chris Larsen's approach to marketing and client engagement offers a masterclass in balancing authenticity with scalability. By leveraging technology, building a robust platform, and tailoring his message to different audience segments, he has created a system that not only attracts clients but also keeps them engaged and satisfied.

As Larsen aptly puts it, "You need to build a platform, provide value, and engage people." For entrepreneurs seeking to get noticed, his strategies provide a roadmap to success.

SCAN TO LISTEN

 **CHRIS LARSEN**

Chapter Two
Consumer Trials.

Melissa Snover
Founder and CEO of Get Nourish3d Ltd, Birmingham, UK

"I focused on what I knew I could do with hard work and a lot of elbow grease."

Innovating the World's First 3D Printed Nutritional Gummies

#GetNourish3d #PersonalizedNutrition #3DPrintedVitamins
#InnovativeHealth #StartupJourney #VeganSupplements #SugarFree
#DigitalMarketing #ConsumerTrust #HealthTech

Introduction

In the bustling city of Birmingham, far from her native New York, Melissa Snover has created a whole new product category through a combination of innovation and careful business plan execution. As the founder and CEO of Nourish3d, Snover has pioneered the 3D printing of personalised nutritional gummies, a venture that has won consumer acclaim and which was the Winner of the King's Award for Enterprise, 2023 Innovation.

The Genesis of Nourish3d

The inception of Nourish3d is rooted in a moment of frustration and a flash of inspiration. Snover, who was already immersed in the world of additive manufacturing for confectionery, found herself grappling with the inconvenience of carrying multiple vitamin bottles during her extensive travels.

"I was in Germany, going through fast-track security at Dusseldorf airport, and my Ziploc bag of vitamins exploded all over the floor. I thought, there's got to be a better way to do this," Snover recalls.

This incident sparked the idea of using 3D printing technology to create personalised nutrition solutions. On her flight back, she sketched the initial concept on a napkin, which would eventually evolve into the innovative Nourish3d stacks available today.

Building the Brand from Scratch

Launching a new product is never easy, and Snover's journey was no exception. Unlike many competitors who outsource manufacturing, Nourish3d built its own food factory, investing heavily in machinery, raw materials, and packaging. This approach left little budget for traditional marketing campaigns.

"We had to focus on what we could do with hard work and a lot of elbow grease, which was to covet the media," Snover explains.

Snover and her team sent samples to media outlets, leveraged social media platforms like LinkedIn, Facebook, and Instagram, and engaged with small but highly engaged communities, such as vegan and keto diet enthusiasts. This grassroots approach helped them gain initial traction without a hefty marketing budget.

Navigating Compliance and Regulation

One of the significant challenges in the food industry is compliance with stringent regulations. Snover's prior experience in large-scale manufacturing equipped her with the knowledge to navigate these complexities.

"Our facilities are FSSC 22,000 certified, the same level as Unilever or Mondelez. It's a massive barrier for people starting out in food," she notes.

Nourish3d conducts rigorous testing to ensure product safety and efficacy, a practice that Snover believes is not sufficiently highlighted in the industry. Despite the high costs and ongoing nature of these compliance measures, they are crucial for maintaining consumer trust and product integrity.

Harnessing the Power of Social Proof

In today's digital age, social proof is a powerful tool for building brand credibility. For a new company like Nourish3d, garnering authentic customer reviews was essential.

"We went until probably the end of April of the first year of trading, contacting every person who purchased, getting their really authentic and honest feedback," Snover shares.

By the end of their first few months, Nourish3d had amassed enough positive reviews to be named the UK's number one customer-rated vitamin and nutrition product. This accolade significantly boosted their marketing efforts, driving organic traffic and customer referrals.

The Role of Influencers and Ambassadors

While many brands rely on paid influencers to promote their products, Snover has taken a different approach. She believes in the power of genuine customer advocacy over paid endorsements.

"We have never paid an influencer to talk about our product. I think it's totally fake. It bothers me when I see other brands do it," she asserts.

Instead, Nourish3d has developed an ambassador programme that allows satisfied customers to share their experiences and earn a small commission for referrals. This strategy not only fosters genuine endorsements but also builds a community of loyal brand advocates.

Learning from Mistakes

Snover's journey has not been without its missteps. One notable example was an early attempt to use television advertising to raise brand awareness.

"TV was very expensive, and it made no difference whatsoever. You need a ton of money and a very consistent long-term campaign to make a difference on TV," she reflects.

This experience taught Snover the importance of focusing on core strengths and the value of digital marketing channels, which offer more measurable and cost-effective results.

"When you're starting something new and certainly when you're doing something no one has ever done before, you have to make the mistakes because there's no case study that I can look at. No book, there's no guidebook. There's no dummies guide to how to build a 3D printing nutrition business. We are really comfortable with failing, and we actually have something in our Friday meetings where we do 'Failure Brags' and we celebrate failure."

Conclusion

Melissa Snover's story is a compelling example of how technology can enable personalisation at scale. When it comes to getting noticed, Snover is clear about the best way to market Nourish3d.

"I think real customers are the best ambassadors and spokespeople of our brand."

SCAN TO LISTEN

 MELISSA SNOVER

Chapter Three
Fractional Sales.

Ray Zamora
President and Founder, Sales Manager Now, Auburn,
Sacramento, California, USA

"When I said I was going to write the book, I was certain I would. It took me five years, but I didn't care; I knew it would be done."

Maximising Sales Revenue for Companies

#FractionalSalesManagement #SalesManagerNow #B2BSales
#SmallBusinessGrowth #SalesStrategy #CustomerEngagement
#SalesLeadership #BusinessMarketing #EntrepreneurialSuccess
#PersonalValuesInBusiness

Introduction

Scaling a business comes with its own set of challenges. As a company grows, it needs to generate leads at a faster rate than its overall growth. Rene Zamora, from Sacramento, California, and founder of Sales Manager Now, offers a scalable solution with fractional sales management. Zamora provides valuable insights into how small businesses can overcome sales hurdles and achieve sustainable growth.

The Concept of Fractional Sales Management

Fractional sales management is a relatively novel concept that addresses a critical gap in small businesses. As companies grow, they often reach a point where they need the expertise of a seasoned sales director but cannot afford one full-time. This is where Zamora's approach comes into play.

"We just get in there and lead the sales teams," says Zamora. "We fraction out our time and skills, working with three to seven businesses at one time. The benefit for the small business is that they only pay us a fraction of our total fees and get the experience they are not usually able to attract."

This model allows small businesses to leverage the expertise of senior sales managers without the financial burden of a full-time hire. It also provides a dynamic and challenging environment for the sales managers, making the work more engaging and rewarding.

Overcoming the Sales Dilemma

Many business owners find themselves hitting a ceiling, unable to push past a certain level of growth. Zamora refers to this as the "small business sales dilemma." He explains that business owners often try various approaches, such as hiring new leaders or promoting from within, but still struggle to find the right solution.

"The owners that come to us are the ones that have tried different approaches. They've tried to hire that leader, bring another manager, or promote a salesperson to a manager. They've changed the team and realised they can't find the answer on their own," Zamora notes. "It's usually people seeking a new answer, and we're fortunate that we're solving some problems for them."

Ensuring Confidentiality and Integrity

One of the primary concerns for business owners considering fractional sales management is confidentiality. Zamora addresses this by ensuring all legal measures, such as non-disclosure agreements, are in place. He also highlights the importance of integrity in maintaining client trust.

"We aren't just taking trade secrets from one and passing them on to another. I think we've earned the integrity with our clients," he asserts. This commitment to confidentiality and ethical conduct is crucial in building and maintaining a reputable business.

Setting Up a Professional Sales Organisation

Transitioning from a founder-led sales approach to a professional sales organisation requires clear expectations and accountability. Zamora emphasises the importance of setting clear goals and ensuring that everyone understands their role in achieving them.

"Expectations are number one. Everyone wants an accountable environment, but you can't have any accountability if you don't have clear expectations understood and agreed on," he explains. "It's not just a goal anymore. A goal is nice to get; a job requirement is to meet this number."

He also stresses the importance of monitoring progress, allowing team members to solve their own problems, and celebrating successes. These fundamentals, often encapsulated in a sales playbook, are essential for a well-functioning sales team.

The Role of Reputation in Sales

Building a strong reputation and brand is vital for any business, and it significantly impacts the effectiveness of the sales team. Zamora shares a simple yet effective strategy he used when starting his consulting business: sending a postcard in advance of a phone call.

"I just sent out a simple little postcard to people I was going to do a phone call on. And then I called them, but I never asked about the postcard," he recalls. "I was listening for the person who said, 'Oh, I think I got your card.' All the ones that didn't, I never mentioned it. But the ones that remembered it, then they took my conversation."

This approach helped to establish a connection and make the initial conversation smoother, demonstrating the power of minor marketing efforts in building a brand and reputation.

Aligning Sales and Marketing

Ensuring alignment between sales and marketing teams is a common challenge, especially in larger companies. Zamora believes that effective communication is key to overcoming this issue.

"You need a leader that can facilitate that conversation to make sure both parties are heard," he advises. "With sales and marketing, you need to understand the other's role in the overall company goal. You can't do every idea, but once you start talking in a business framework, the exaggeration and drama go down."

He also suggests implementing an all-employee bonus system to align everyone's efforts towards common goals. This approach fosters a sense of unity and shared purpose, motivating the entire team to strive for success.

Transparency and Empowerment

Sharing business information transparently can empower employees and foster a sense of partnership. Zamora encourages business owners to share as much information as they are comfortable with, as it builds trust and engagement.

"The more business information you share with people, the more you empower them," he says. "It tells that employee that, 'Oh, I'm trusted with this.' It's almost like making them a little bit of a partner."

The Journey of an Entrepreneur

Zamora's journey as an entrepreneur is a testament to the power of seeking clarity and staying authentic to one's passion. He describes how the idea of fractional sales management came to him after a period of seeking spiritual guidance.

"After about six months of prayer, someone suggested, 'Why don't you just become a fractional sales manager for small businesses?' It was like the bright lights came on," he recalls. "The next day, I owned it. I domained it. A week later, I had my first client."

Since then, Zamora has successfully grown his business, never wanting for clients and continually finding new ways to get noticed, such as writing a book and participating in podcasts.

Conclusion

Rene Zamora's insights into fractional sales management offer a practical and effective solution for small businesses looking to scale their sales operations. By leveraging experienced sales managers on a part-time basis, businesses can overcome growth hurdles without the financial burden of a full-time hire. Key take aways include the importance of clear expectations, effective communication, and building a strong reputation.

As Zamora aptly puts it, "The more business information you share with people, the more you empower them." This ethos of transparency and empowerment is crucial for any business seeking to achieve sustainable growth.

SCAN TO LISTEN

 ## RENE
ZAMORA

Chapter Four
A Shared Mission.

Surendra Singh
PR & Marketing Manager, ViAct, Hong Kong

"We make our customers our brand ambassadors."

AI-Enabled Facilities Monitoring and Management

#ViAct #ConstructionTech #AIConstruction #ESGCompliance
#UserGeneratedContent #BrandAmbassadors #DigitalMarketing
#SustainabilityInConstruction #VideoTestimonials
#InnovativeMarketing

Introduction

In the dynamic world of construction technology, getting noticed can be a formidable challenge. Surendra Singh, the Head of Public Relations and Marketing at ViAct, a Hong Kong-based AI-driven construction technology company, shares his strategies and insights on how to effectively market a niche B2B SaaS product.

The Unique Proposition of ViAct

Founded in 2016, ViAct has quickly established itself as a leader in AI-based construction technology. Founded by Gary Ng and Hugo Cheuk in Hong Kong, ViAct positions itself as Asia's top sustainability-focused AI company that provides "Scenario-based Vision Intelligence" solutions for risk-prone workplaces, including construction, oil and gas, manufacturing, facility management, and mining industry, to build smart cities and nations. The company has successfully deployed its solutions in over 50 projects across Asia and the Middle East. Singh attributes this success to their unique scenario-based AI algorithms, which set them apart from competitors.

"We are making our users, our customers, our brand ambassadors," Singh explains. "We believe in the feedback we are getting from the people who are deploying our solution."

Customer Engagement: Turning Users into Brand Ambassadors

One of the key strategies Singh employs is transforming customers into brand ambassadors. This approach leverages the positive experiences of existing users to build credibility and trust in the market.

"We are not just talking about our product; we are making our customers our brand ambassadors," Singh says. "If you see the feedback from CMAX Venture, Autodesk, and AECOM, the people who believed in us are saying that this is something different."

To achieve this, ViAct collects feedback through manual processes and video testimonials. Singh acknowledges the challenges of confidentiality and security but emphasises the importance of aligning with the broader purpose of Environmental, Social, and Governance (ESG) in construction projects.

"Our product ensures a complete 360-degree ecosystem for ESG in construction projects," Singh notes. "They are comfortable with us because we are not just focusing on safety and productivity but also on the environment."

Practical Steps for Gathering Testimonials

Singh shares practical steps for gathering customer testimonials, which are crucial for building a brand. ViAct's team is on the ground in key locations like Singapore and Hong Kong, recording video testimonials directly from customers. In regions where the team is not present, they conduct virtual one-on-one meetings to capture feedback.

"We have a one-on-one virtual conversation and get their feedback," Singh explains. "We use SurveyMonkey to get some written feedback, but we believe in short videos to deliver the testimonials."

Leveraging Social Media and Video Platforms

ViAct hosts its testimonial videos on YouTube and its website, using social media platforms to spread the word organically. Singh highlights the importance of a balanced approach between organic marketing and paid advertising.

"60% should be organic and 40% paid," Singh advises. "We are running ads for 365 days with a small budget, targeting specific audiences through LinkedIn ads."

Media Relations and Speaking Events

In addition to social media, ViAct actively participates in industry-specific events and expos. These events provide an opportunity to showcase their product and engage directly with potential customers.

"There are build expos and real estate expos where we display our product," Singh says. "People understand it in 30 seconds."

Internal Communications: A Remote-First Approach

ViAct operates as a remote-first company, with team members spread across Singapore, Hong Kong, India, Vietnam, and Romania. Singh emphasises the importance of effective internal communication to ensure everyone is aligned with the company's goals.

"We use DingTalk for communication and Trello for task management," Singh explains. "Everyone is responsible for what the brand is going to be."

Localisation and Content Distribution

Managing content across multiple geographies and languages is another challenge ViAct navigates adeptly. The content creation is centralised in India, while localisation and distribution are handled by teams in the respective regions.

"We have a team working on translating the contents," Singh says. "We run advertisements in English for the USA and UK, and in Chinese for Hong Kong and other areas."

Conclusion

Surendra Singh's insights offer valuable lessons for entrepreneurs looking to get their business noticed in a niche market. By turning customers into brand ambassadors, leveraging social media, participating in industry events, and maintaining effective internal communication, ViAct has successfully built a strong brand in the construction technology sector.

"Everyone is responsible for what the brand is going to be," Singh concludes, highlighting the collective effort required to build and sustain a successful brand.

SCAN TO LISTEN

 SURENDRA SINGH

Chapter Five
Engaging Stakeholders.

Timber Barker
CEO/Founder, Boom Interactive, Inc., Sandy, Utah, USA

"It's about getting the community involved from various angles. And that's just me picking up the phone sometimes and calling."

Innovating a Digital Twin Technology for School Safety

#BoomInteractive #DigitalTwins #SchoolSafety #PublicSafetyTech #AI #EmergencyResponse #CommunityEngagement #B2BMarketing #DataPrivacy #InnovativeTech

Introduction

AI is changing the way that we see the world, and how we can represent the world virtually. Timber Barker, CEO of Boom Interactive, is at the forefront of a digital twinning revolution. Based in Sandy, Utah, Boom Interactive is pioneering the use of AI and 3D technology to enhance school safety. Barker recently shared his journey, insights, and strategies for marketing a groundbreaking product in a highly regulated environment.

The Genesis of Boom Interactive's School Safety Solution

Timber Barker's journey began with the development of an AI-based platform that creates digital twins from flat floor plans. Initially aimed at the design and film industries, the technology soon found a new and critical application in school safety. "One of my investors suggested that our technology could be invaluable for schools to share floor plans with first responders," Barker recalls. This idea led to a collaboration with a prominent school district in Arizona, where the technology was met with enthusiasm.

The platform allows schools to create 3D models of their buildings, complete with blind corners, furniture layouts, and real-time updates. This information can be shared with first responders, providing them with crucial data during emergencies. "We can bring in actual CCTV footage and show where cameras are placed on a 3D plane," Barker explains. "This helps first responders get to where they need to go faster than anyone else."

Overcoming Regulatory Hurdles

Marketing an AI product in a regulatory environment is no small feat. Barker acknowledges the challenges but emphasises the importance of community involvement. "We go to all leaders – city officials, superintendents, and local police departments," he says. By engaging multiple stakeholders, Boom Interactive ensures that their product meets the needs of various groups.

One of the primary concerns from schools was the security of camera feeds. "They asked if there was a way to shut off the camera feeds after a certain time," Barker notes. Boom Interactive addressed this by allowing schools to control access to the feeds, similar to how Google Docs permissions work. Another concern was the potential misuse of floor plans. Barker points out that such information is already accessible through other means, such as city records or scanning apps. "We need to train and teach leaders on how to use this technology responsibly," he asserts.

The Power of Listening

A key strategy for Boom Interactive has been listening to their users. "We listen, and if someone says, 'It would be really good if you could archive it in this way,' we take that feedback seriously," Barker says. This approach has allowed the company to refine their product based on real-world needs. For instance, the city of Glendale provided valuable feedback that led to new features and improvements.

Marketing and Distribution Strategies

Boom Interactive employs a dual strategy for marketing and distribution. While they have a direct sales team, they also explore partnerships with security companies that already have established client bases. "We're talking to a big security company that has clients already," Barker reveals. This approach allows Boom Interactive to leverage existing distribution channels while also building their brand.

The company's technology is designed to be user-friendly and scalable. "If every school called us tomorrow, we could have accounts set up and running instantly," Barker states. The platform is cross-platform, working on iOS, Android, Mac, and Windows, making it accessible to a wide range of users.

Building the Corporate Brand

Balancing multiple product lines can be challenging, but Boom Interactive has managed to do so by focusing on their core technology. "We started off wanting to be nerds and create an engine to license out," Barker says. However, as they developed prototypes and demos, they realised that they had full-fledged products. The company now offers three products, all built on the same underlying technology. This allows them to quickly adapt and customise their solutions for different industries.

Conclusion

Timber Barker's journey with Boom Interactive offers valuable lessons for entrepreneurs. By engaging multiple stakeholders, listening to user feedback, and leveraging existing distribution channels, Boom Interactive has successfully introduced a groundbreaking product in a highly regulated environment.

The key take away? Involve your community and listen to their needs. As Barker puts it, "This isn't easy, but it's been fun and exciting to see people light up when they see it."

SCAN TO LISTEN

 ## TIMBER
BARKER

Chapter Six
Profitable Relationships.

Abhishek Kaushik

*Co-founder & CEO @ WeCP | Forbes Technology Council,
We Create Problems was founded in Nov 2015, San Francisco,
California, USA*

"It's about how well you understand and solve the customer's problems, creating value not just through your products but through your insights and relationships."

Transforming the Technical Recruitment Industry

#WeCP #TechnicalRecruitment #CommunityBuilding
#ReferralMarketing #ContentDevelopment #HiringSolutions
#TechIndustry #SEO #LeadGeneration #GlobalExpansion

Introduction

Now based in San Francisco, Abhishek Kaushik, CEO and founder of We Create Problems (WCP), is revolutionising the recruitment process in highly skilled industries. His company, founded in the tech hub of Bangalore, India, is a technical hiring platform and community streamlining the recruitment process for engineering talent.

The Genesis of We Create Problems

We Create Problems, or WCP, is a platform designed to simplify the technical hiring process. "We help talent acquisition leaders screen candidates by coding assignments, projects, and technical questions, interview them face-to-face, and onboard them in one click," Abhishek explains. This comprehensive approach has attracted clients like Microsoft and other blue-chip companies, a testament to the platform's efficacy.

Building a Brand from Scratch

Starting a business without substantial marketing funds can be daunting. Abhishek and his team adopted a grassroots approach, leveraging customer referrals to build their client base. "We asked our customers, 'Why did you trust us? What do you like in us? And if you like us, can you refer us to a couple of your colleagues?'" This strategy proved effective, with each new customer often leading to another.

The Power of Community

Recognising the importance of community, Abhishek launched technical-hiring.com, a platform for technical hiring leaders worldwide. "The objective behind building this community was to educate most of the hiring leaders to learn technical hiring," he says. Inspired by Canva's mission to democratise design, Abhishek aims to empower recruiters to hire engineers without needing to be engineers themselves.

Addressing Market Needs

Abhishek identified a significant inefficiency in the hiring process: "Nearly 40% of the engineering hours of a company on average is spent on hiring engineers, not shipping product and not writing code." By enabling recruitment teams to handle 95% of the hiring process, WCP aims to free up engineers to focus on their core tasks, thereby reducing revenue loss and improving productivity.

Content-Driven Marketing

Content plays a crucial role in WCP's marketing strategy. Abhishek and his team delve into platforms like GitHub and Stack Overflow to understand the pain points of their target audience. "We collated all the problems on a simple Google sheet and started writing the pain points and around those pain points we started drafting articles," he explains. This methodical approach has resulted in a robust blog community with over 200 articles, generating five to eight marketing qualified leads daily.

Leveraging Technology

WCP utilises a combination of tools to manage their marketing efforts. "We've connected LinkedIn to our HubSpot. We are running on a starter plan on HubSpot, so we don't pay a lot to HubSpot as of now," Abhishek shares. This integration allows them to efficiently capture leads and engage with potential customers through email campaigns and phone calls.

Understanding Customer Needs

A key aspect of WCP's content strategy is addressing the functional, social, and emotional needs of their target audience. For instance, a head of talent acquisition's functional need might be to fill 50 engineering positions by the end of the quarter. Socially, they seek recognition from their organisation, and emotionally, they desire a stress-free hiring process. "We say, look, you can hire being happy. You can sleep peacefully while we hire for you," Abhishek notes.

Expanding Globally

As WCP expands its footprint to the USA and the UK, Abhishek emphasises the importance of effective marketing strategies. "We have created three simple strategies in marketing: positioning, lead generation, and branding," he says. By focusing on these areas, WCP aims to build a strong global presence.

Building Customer Relationships

Customer engagement is at the heart of WCP's strategy. Abhishek believes in building friendships with customers, fostering a sense of trust and collaboration. "A good customer is a great customer when he's sharing your problems with you, without even asking," he asserts. This approach has led to customers willingly sharing their positive experiences on their social media handles, further enhancing WCP's brand.

Conclusion

Abhishek Kaushik's journey with We Create Problems offers a masterclass in effective marketing and brand building. By focusing on customer referrals, community engagement, content-driven strategies, and understanding customer needs, WCP has successfully carved a niche in the competitive technical hiring market.

The key take away for entrepreneurs is the importance of building genuine relationships with customers and leveraging their feedback to drive growth.

SCAN TO LISTEN

 ## ABHISHEK KAUSHIK

Chapter Seven
Partnership Success.

Denis O'Shea

Founder | Microsoft Partner of the Year 2021, Mobile Mentor, Nashville, Tennessee, USA

"I had a hard conversation asking Nokia for support to start something that basically pointed out their product's underutilisation."

Bridging the Gap Between Technology Companies and Phone Users

#MobileMentor #Entrepreneurship #TechInnovation #PartnerStrategy #B2BMarketing #MobileTechnology #CyberSecurity #EndpointEcosystem #GlobalExpansion #StrategicPartnerships

Introduction

In the world of entrepreneurship, the ability to forge strategic partnerships can be the difference between obscurity and success. Denis O'Shea, originally from New Zealand and now based in Nashville, Tennessee, exemplifies this principle through his company, Mobile Mentor. Founded in 2004, Mobile Mentor has grown to serve customers across multiple continents, thanks to O'Shea's knack for building powerful alliances.

Identifying a Market Need

Denis O'Shea's journey began in the early 2000s while working for Nokia. He noticed a significant gap in the market: despite the advanced capabilities of smartphones, most users were only utilising them for basic functions like calls and texts. "Companies like Nokia were producing these amazing smartphones, and people were not using them for what they were intended," O'Shea recalls. This observation led him to leave Nokia and establish Mobile Mentor, a company dedicated to helping users unlock the full potential of their smartphones.

The Bold Pitch

O'Shea's first major move was to approach his former employer, Nokia, with a bold proposition. He sought funding to start his new venture, arguing that it would ultimately benefit Nokia by increasing smartphone usage. "I said, look, I've had 15 great years working with you. I'd like to leave and set up a company, and I'd like you to give me some money to do so," he recounts. Surprisingly, Nokia agreed, providing the initial capital to get Mobile Mentor off the ground.

Next, O'Shea approached Vodafone, the world's largest mobile carrier at the time, with a similar pitch. He proposed a pilot project involving 10,000 users to demonstrate how his service could drive data and voice consumption. Vodafone was convinced, and with the backing of both Nokia and Vodafone, Mobile Mentor was poised for rapid growth.

Expanding Globally

With the support of these industry giants, O'Shea set his sights on international expansion. His strategy was simple yet effective: leverage influential New Zealanders in target markets to form partnerships with local mobile carriers. "We found a really influential New Zealander in Brazil who was able to get us to senior people in a mobile carrier called Telecom Italia," O'Shea explains. This approach was replicated in China and Australia, allowing Mobile Mentor to establish a presence in these significant markets.

Co-Branding for Success

One of the key strategies that propelled Mobile Mentor to success was co-branding with local carriers. In Australia, for example, the service was branded as Telstra Mentor, combining the strength of Telstra's brand with Mobile Mentor's expertise. "They promoted the service on radio, on TV. They even created a little box that they put in their retail shop," O'Shea notes. This co-branding not only increased visibility but also lent credibility to Mobile Mentor's offerings.

The American Dream

Expanding into the American market presented a new set of challenges. O'Shea decided to focus on a specific niche: healthcare in Nashville, Tennessee. "We picked Nashville, Tennessee, because it's such a big healthcare city," he says. By joining local organisations and networking extensively, O'Shea eventually secured a deal with the Hospital Corporation of America, the largest hospital company in the USA. "It was about two years of networking to get that first deal. But once I got the first deal, then I had arrived," he reflects.

Creating a New Category

Always the innovator, O'Shea recognised the need to differentiate Mobile Mentor in a crowded market. He decided to create a new category called the "endpoint ecosystem," focusing on the myriad devices and software that remote workers use daily. "We thought we need to freshen up this conversation if we're going to get attention and if we're going to cut through all the noise in this marketplace," he explains. By conducting nationwide research and making the data freely available, Mobile Mentor garnered significant media attention and established itself as a thought leader in this new category.

Leveraging Awards for Credibility

Winning awards can significantly boost a company's credibility, and Mobile Mentor is no exception. In 2021, the company won the Microsoft Partner of the Year award, a recognition that had a profound impact on their business. "The amount of PR and attention we got from that was beyond anything I could ever describe," O'Shea says. This accolade opened doors to new opportunities and partnerships, further solidifying Mobile Mentor's reputation.

The Art of Partnership

O'Shea attributes much of his success to his ability to form meaningful partnerships. "It's about understanding them and what are the outcomes they're looking for and making the partnership about enabling them to achieve their goals," he advises. By aligning with partners' objectives and demonstrating deep empathy for their business needs, Mobile Mentor has been able to build strong, mutually beneficial relationships.

Conclusion

Denis O'Shea's journey with Mobile Mentor underscores the power of strategic partnerships in building a successful business. From leveraging co-branding opportunities to creating new market categories and winning prestigious awards, O'Shea's story offers valuable lessons for entrepreneurs.

The key take away? Focus on understanding and aligning with your partners' goals to create lasting, impactful relationships.

SCAN TO LISTEN

 # DENIS O'SHEA

Chapter Eight
Launching a TV Show.

Heidi Dugan

TV Host | Celebrity | Award Winning Influencer | Author | Governance | Business Growth Strategist | Award Winning Leading Woman in Business Founder, Shanghai, China

"I think that if you've got something that you want to share and you are authentic about that, and you're consistent with that, people will naturally start to follow, and they'll be fascinated with that journey."

Creating Access to the Chinese Consumer

#HeidiDugan #Arete #PersonalBranding #InfluencerMarketing #ChinaBusiness #InternationalTrade #CrossBorderCommerce #BrandVisibility #SocialMediaStrategy #WomenEntrepreneurs

Introduction

Heidi Dugan, an Australian entrepreneur based in Shanghai, has carved out a unique niche in China's competitive market. With her multimedia wellness and food business, Areté, she has successfully transitioned from obscurity to recognition and fame. In a recent conversation, Heidi shared her journey, offering valuable insights into brand building, social media strategies, customer engagement, and media relations.

Building a Brand in a Foreign Land

Heidi's journey in China began 26 years ago, and she has spent the majority of that time on television. As the first foreign TV host in China, she created a show called "You Are the Chef," which became immensely popular. The show featured Heidi visiting hotels and restaurants, interacting with chefs, and teaching viewers about Western and Chinese cuisines.

Reflecting on her success, Heidi emphasised the importance of consistency. "The real success was that we did one show for so many years and the method we used and the format that we used was exactly the same every single day. We just changed the recipes," she explained. This consistency helped build a loyal audience who knew what to expect and kept coming back for more.

Overcoming Challenges

Starting a business in China comes with its own set of challenges, especially for a foreigner. Heidi's initial struggle was the language barrier, which limited her opportunities. However, she turned this challenge into an advantage by becoming a guest host on various shows, which expanded her reach and visibility.

Heidi's breakthrough came when she received a licence to be the first foreign host on Chinese TV. "I was at the right place at the right time to be able to be fortunate enough to get that. I'm highly aware that being able to live broadcast on national TV is something that has only been permitted me because of the years of trust that I've built up with the government, with the Chinese consumer and the public," she noted.

Leveraging Visibility

Areté, Heidi's business, capitalises on her visibility and relationships. She believes in the power of being visible across various platforms, whether it's TV, social media, or events. "Visibility, I suppose, is the one core thing for me that I'm always thinking of," she said. This visibility allows companies to connect with her and access her followers, creating a mutually beneficial relationship.

Heidi also highlighted the importance of repurposing content across different channels. "I definitely have two different markets. One is the international brands and what we do globally and how we get visibility from that. And that's very much all the social media platforms," she explained. For the Chinese market, she uses platforms like WeChat, Douyin, Weibo, and traditional media to reach her audience.

Authenticity and Consistency

Heidi's success is also attributed to her authenticity and consistency. She believes that being true to oneself and passionate about the topic can naturally attract an audience. "If you've got something that you want to share and you're authentic about that and you're consistent with that, people will naturally start to follow and they'll be fascinated with that journey," she said.

However, maintaining consistency can be challenging for entrepreneurs who are always brimming with new ideas. Heidi admitted that her biggest obstacle was staying focused on one thing. To overcome this, she brought in a Chief Operating Officer (COO) to provide structure and keep her on track. "The only way that I could overcome that was to bring in an awesome COO that goes, no, no, no, we're going to do it this way. And you're going to continue doing it. You're just going to get better at it," she shared.

Strategic Partnerships

Heidi's approach to managing her business is to keep it lean and partner with the best companies. This strategy allows her to focus on her core competencies while outsourcing other tasks. "I partner with amazing companies that can do everything that I need them to do. And then I don't spend the time having to work with a huge number of employees and employee issues," she explained.

These partnerships are mutually beneficial, as Heidi ensures that her partners also gain from the collaboration. "Anyone that I work with, even if we're paying them for the job that they're doing, is that I want to make sure that they are better off when we leave or as we continue," she said.

Future Endeavours

Heidi is excited about her new brand, Rise. This is Living, which focuses on wellness and aims to give people the confidence to take control of their health and happiness. The brand will launch in China and collaborate with various health and wellness brands. "We're launching it in December here in China. And we're working with so many fantastic health and wellness brands," she revealed.

Conclusion

Entrepreneurs can take away the importance of visibility, creating content, and being consistent.

"If you've got something that you want to share and you're authentic about that and you're consistent with that, people will naturally start to follow, and they'll be fascinated with that journey."

SCAN TO LISTEN

 ## HEIDI
DUGAN

Actionable Insights

1. Develop Authenticity in Personal Branding
   Focus on being genuine about your interests and expertise. Share your journey openly and authentically to build trust and engagement. This honest approach will attract a loyal audience over time.

2. Consistently Deliver Content
   Stick to a consistent content schedule while keeping the format familiar to the audience, as predictability can foster a comforting viewing or participation habit. Regularity helps maintain and grow viewer engagement.

3. Utilise Strategic Visibility
   Enhance your public visibility through various platforms such as TV, social media, and public events. Regular appearances keep you and your brand in the public eye, crucial for gathering a broad audience.

4. Capitalise on Networking Opportunities

   Maintain and grow a robust network. Strong relationships can lead to new business opportunities, partnerships, and increased brand visibility.

5. Leverage Influencer Partnerships

   Connect with other influencers to tap into their followers, thereby amplifying your visibility. This strategic partnership can introduce your brand to diverse audiences.

6. Engage with Local Cultures and Trends

   Adapt your business and personal brand to resonate with local preferences and cultural trends. Understanding and integrating into the local context can significantly boost acceptance and success.

7. Diversify Media Platforms

   Do not limit your promotions to one medium. Explore various platforms like traditional media, online platforms, and live events to reach a wider audience.

8. Offer Consistent Value with Innovations

   Maintain core themes or services but innovate with new offerings based on audience feedback and market trends. This balance keeps content fresh yet reliable.

9. Expand Sectoral Influence

   Diversify your influence into various sectors by leveraging your foundational brand. This expansion can lead to broader business opportunities and increase overall market presence.

10. Initiate Engagement with Local and Global Markets

    Utilise your platform to interact with both local and international markets. Understand and employ strategies tailored to each demographic to maximise brand impact and growth.

Chapter Nine
All About People.

Tim Ringel
Global CEO, Meet the People, New York, New York, USA

"I have learned, and I didn't value that early on, that helping people is how you build relationships and how your network is going to work."

Building a Global Advertising Network

#MeetThePeople #TimRingel #GlobalMarketing #Entrepreneurship #ProgrammaticAdvertising #ClientEngagement #BusinessScaling #CorporateCulture #StrategicAcquisitions #MarketingInnovation

Introduction

Tim Ringel, a German entrepreneur now residing in New York, has built a formidable reputation in the advertising industry. As the CEO of Meet the People, a company that has grown from zero to over 500 employees in less than a year, Ringel's journey offers invaluable insights for entrepreneurs striving to get their businesses noticed. His experience spans multiple continents and industries, making his strategies and lessons particularly relevant for today's global market.

The Early Days: Hustling for the First Client

Starting a business is never easy and getting that first client can be the most challenging part. Ringel's journey began in Germany when he was just 21 years old. "I started my business knowing nothing about business," he recalls. "Being 21, still in college, working a job as an IT administrator in a large bank because I knew computers really well."

Ringel's initial strategy was straightforward but effective: cold calling and sending letters. "At that time, there was no LinkedIn in 1999, 1998. So you really had to work really hard to convince people that you are an upcoming innovative company that can help them solve something," he explains. His persistence paid off, and he managed to get his foot in the door by identifying mistakes on potential clients' websites and offering solutions.

The Power of Authenticity in Client Acquisition

In today's digital age, the personal touch can often be lost amidst automated emails and social media outreach. However, Ringel believes that authenticity still holds significant value. "Something that is authentic and different is going to resonate really well, especially when you're an upcoming company because it shows that you care," he says.

Ringel's approach to client acquisition has evolved but remains rooted in personal engagement. "Even in a large assignment, a personal touch still goes a long way with a VP of marketing, SVP of marketing, whatever that is. That personal relationship is still very, very important," he emphasises.

Scaling with Authenticity

Managing a large-scale operation while maintaining a personal touch is a challenge many entrepreneurs face. Ringel's solution lies in decentralisation. "Each of the brands we acquire remains independent within the structure. We own them outright, but each of them has their own DNA, their own authentic approach to how to talk to clients," he explains.

This strategy allows Meet the People to scale without losing the personal touch that clients value. "We have multiple leaders within the business that win business and talk to clients with a very personal touch," Ringel adds.

Creating a Unified Vision

While each brand under Meet the People operates independently, Ringel ensures that they are united by a common vision. "When you are a small company, you have really two options. You can either build a very, very clear vision for your team that people can rally behind, or you can create an enemy," he says.

Ringel's approach involves both strategies. "Creating the enemy is picking a competitor that you want to beat on winning business, on being better. It helps people to rally behind something that might be really blurry," he explains. This dual approach has helped Ringel create a cohesive culture across his diverse portfolio of companies.

Navigating Investor Relations

Securing investment is a critical aspect of scaling any business. Ringel categorises potential investors into four types: business angels, family offices, venture capital, and private equity. Each type requires a different approach. "Business angel capital is very emotional money, network-related, very emotional, small tickets that ideally give you strategic advantage," he notes.

For Meet the People, Ringel chose private equity. "Private equity money does not necessarily care so much about the vision. They care much more about, is there an established industry that you are disrupting?" he explains. This pragmatic approach aligns with the service-based nature of his business, which relies on "walking assets" – people rather than machines.

Programmatic Advertising: A Two-Pronged Approach

As an expert in programmatic advertising, Ringel offers two key pieces of advice for entrepreneurs. First, focus on search. "If you can't make it work on search, aka Google, on an ROI that you need for your business, you will never make it on social," he asserts. The intent data from search is far more valuable than the network data from social media.

Second, implement a loyalty programme from the outset. "Don't try to acquire your customer twice. Start immediately with a loyalty programme, especially when you're consumer-facing," he advises. This strategy helps businesses avoid paying "ransom" to big tech platforms for reacquiring customers they already have.

Conclusion

Tim Ringel's journey from a young entrepreneur in Germany to the CEO of a rapidly growing company in New York offers a masterclass in getting noticed. His strategies – ranging from authentic client engagement to effective investor relations and programmatic advertising – provide actionable insights for entrepreneurs at any stage.

As Ringel succinctly puts it, "If you don't work hard, if you don't do it yourself in the beginning, nobody's going to do it."

SCAN TO LISTEN

 TIM
RINGEL

Chapter Ten
Community Sales.

Yong-Soo Chung
Founder, Urban EveryDay Carry, San Francisco, California, USA

"Wow, I can't believe you actually listened to what I said and implemented it."

Building an E-Commerce Empire in Everyday Carry

#UrbanEDC #EverydayCarry #NicheMarket #DirectToConsumer
#ProductDrops #CommunityBuilding #CustomerEngagement
#Entrepreneurship #Craftsmanship #CustomerFeedback

Introduction

Yong-Soo Chung has carved out a niche with his company, Urban Everyday Carry (Urban EDC). EDC products are those which people buy and take around with them, including pocketknives, torches, key holders, etc.

His journey from a one-bedroom apartment to an eight-figure business in San Francisco offers invaluable lessons for entrepreneurs striving to get their businesses noticed. Here, we distil the essence of his insights on brand building, social media, customer engagement, and more.

Humbling Beginnings

Yong-Soo's story begins in 2015, in a modest one-bedroom apartment in San Francisco. He launched Urban EDC with high hopes, having built an Instagram following of 10,000.

However, his initial foray into e-commerce was met with silence.

"I thought I was ready to launch the shop with 10,000 followers... but it was like crickets, just nothing," he recalls. This humbling experience taught him a crucial lesson: a large social media following does not necessarily translate into sales.

The Importance of the Right Audience

Yong-Soo quickly realised that his initial audience was not his target market. "A common mistake that a lot of entrepreneurs make is that they build an audience and then think they can convert that audience into paying customers," he explains. His initial followers were interested in the images he posted, not the products he was selling.

To rectify this, he focused on understanding his core audience. "Each week, we drop new inventory... and just listen to the customers and gather valuable feedback," he says. This iterative process of listening and adapting helped him home in on what his customers truly wanted.

Building a Passionate Community

Urban EDC specialises in everyday carry items – wallets, phones, flashlights, and bottle openers. These are not just functional items but are part of a passionate community that loves to showcase their gear. "There's a really passionate community of everyday carry people who show off what they carry today," says Yong-Soo.

To engage this community, Chung implemented a strategy of weekly gear drops. "We have weekly gear drops that sell out very quickly... people start talking, right? They tell their friends, Hey, this shop is... selling out in five seconds," he explains. This created a buzz and a sense of urgency, driving more traffic to his site.

Leveraging Feedback Loops

One of the key strategies Chung employed was the use of feedback loops. "Our company lives on Slack... we use a simple survey company called Typeform, and we have the surveys ported directly into a separate Slack channel using Zapier," he explains. This ensured that all feedback was visible to the entire team, fostering a culture of accountability and continuous improvement.

"Everything just comes in... you can't hide behind bad feedback," he emphasises. This transparency allowed Urban EDC to make incremental improvements based on real customer input, building a loyal following over time.

Consistency Is Key

Yong-Soo stresses the importance of consistency in building a brand. "When someone subscribes to your emailing list or starts following you on Instagram, they have a certain expectation of what they're going to get from you," he says. For Urban EDC, this meant consistently delivering new gear every Wednesday, meeting customer expectations, and building trust.

Empowering Creators

Urban EDC is not just a marketplace; it is a platform for creators and designers. "We want to empower designers and makers to really get their creativity out into the wild," says Yong-Soo. This focus on community and empowerment has created a symbiotic relationship where consumers often become creators.

"Someone that starts off as a consumer... ends up buying some machinery and starts making their own gear," he notes. This cycle of empowerment has been a cornerstone of Urban EDC's success.

The B2B Venture: Growth Jet

Yong-Soo's entrepreneurial spirit doesn't stop at Urban EDC. He also founded Growth Jet, a climate-neutral certified logistics company. "We're actually the first third-party logistics company in the world to become climate neutral certified," he proudly states.

The challenges in the B2B space are different. "A lot of these companies love the fact that we care about the environment... but they don't share our name to other competitors," he explains. Word of mouth has been the primary growth driver for Growth Jet, underscoring the importance of delivering exceptional service.

A Unified Framework

Despite the differences between his B2C and B2B ventures, Yong-Soo believes in a unified approach centred around feedback loops. "The most important thing are these feedback loops... you will hear from the customers, whether or not they enjoy something," he says. Implementing customer feedback not only improves the product but also builds loyalty.

Conclusion

Yong-Soo Chung's journey from a one-bedroom apartment to an eight-figure business is a testament to the power of understanding your audience, leveraging feedback, and maintaining consistency. This relentless focus on customer engagement and incremental improvement is the key take away for any entrepreneur.

As Yong-Soo puts it, "It's all about consistency... week after week, they're on the website because each Wednesday, we're going to drop new gear."

SCAN TO LISTEN

 YONG SOO CHUNG

Chapter Eleven
Being Yourself.

Mark Asquith

"That British Podcast Guy," MD & Co-founder of Captivate, Manchester, UK

"It's about being unequivocally yourself."

Starting, Building, and Selling a World-Leading Podcast Platform

#CaptivatePodcast #MarkAsquith #Podcasting #DigitalMarketing #Entrepreneurship #AudienceGrowth #KeynoteSpeaking #ContentCreation #InnovationInPodcasting #BrandDevelopment

Introduction

In the north west of England city of Manchester, renowned for two football clubs and a vibrant music and media scene, Mark Asquith has put the city on the map in the podcasting world. As the co-founder and managing director of Captivate, a podcast hosting and growth platform, Asquith has overseen its rise from a fledgling startup to a company hosting over 10,000 shows. His journey offers invaluable lessons for entrepreneurs seeking to get their businesses noticed.

The Genesis of Captivate

Mark Asquith's foray into podcasting began over a decade ago, at a time when the medium was still in its infancy in the UK. "I've been in podcasting for a decade now, maybe just over a decade," he recalls. His initial ventures included a pop culture podcast and a business podcast, both of which allowed him to apply his background in marketing, branding, and digital design to a new and exciting field.

In 2014, Asquith and his business partner, Kieran McKeefery, launched Podcast Websites, a fully managed WordPress service with integrated audio hosting. This venture laid the groundwork for Captivate, which they launched in 2019. "We just built a business called Podcast Websites, a fully managed WordPress service with integrated audio hosting, which then led to Captivate later," Asquith explains.

Scratching Your Own Itch

One of the key drivers behind Captivate's success has been Asquith's ability to identify and address gaps in the market. "It's the old cliché of just scratching your own itch, really," he says. His deep involvement in the podcasting community, both as a creator and a conference speaker, provided him with first-hand insights into the needs and frustrations of podcasters.

"I was able to kind of ask people, I would just get this immense feedback without asking or trying because people would just say, 'Oh, isn't it annoying that you can't do this?'" he notes. This feedback, combined with his own experience of producing over 1,500 podcast episodes, informed the development of Captivate's features.

The Power of Networking

Asquith's active presence at podcasting conferences, both in the UK and the USA, has been fundamental to Captivate's brand-building success. "Before the lockdowns hit in 2020, we were out in the USA five months of the year, six months of the year at the podcasting conferences," he says. His participation in events like Podcast Movement and Podfest, where he was often one of the few British speakers, helped him build a robust network within the industry.

"My approach to marketing, to networking is the same as my approach to this conversation, which is the same as my approach to a conversation in the bar with my friends, which is to just be unequivocally yourself," Asquith asserts. This authenticity has not only earned him a reputation as a thought leader but also attracted the attention of Global, the media giant that eventually acquired Captivate.

Building a Product That Stands Out

Captivate's success can also be attributed to its focus on creating a product that genuinely meets the needs of its users. "Captivate is built without asking anyone what they wanted," Asquith reveals. Instead of relying on traditional customer research, he and McKeefery focused on building features that they knew would be useful, even if users didn't initially recognise their value.

For instance, Captivate offers a dynamic show notes builder that saves podcasters significant time. "If I were to ask people, 'Would you pay for it?' They would say no, because it's not that much of a problem," Asquith explains. However, by including such features as part of the hosting cost, Captivate has created a comprehensive toolkit that sets it apart from competitors.

The Importance of Passion

For Asquith, the key to getting noticed in any industry is genuine passion. "There's no point starting a podcast unless you can put time into it," he advises. This principle extends to all aspects of business. "If you genuinely love what you do and you give to it, the numbers will naturally come because you will unequivocally be absolutely everywhere and be so well-known that it's impossible for the numbers not to come."

This passion is evident in Asquith's continued involvement in the podcasting community, even after Captivate's acquisition by Global. "I still do support, and I've sold the damn thing, and I still do support," he says. His commitment to the industry and to helping others succeed has been a cornerstone of Captivate's growth.

Conclusion

Mark Asquith's journey with Captivate underscores the importance of passion, authenticity, and a deep understanding of your industry. By immersing himself in the podcasting community and building a product that genuinely meets the needs of its users, Asquith has created a platform that stands out in a crowded market. For entrepreneurs seeking to get their businesses noticed, his story offers a powerful reminder that success comes from loving what you do and giving back to the community you serve.

"I believe it's fundamental to be wholly in the industry that you're in, to give to that industry, and to go and be present at all of the things. And the marketing strategy, marketing tactics, product strategy, product development, brand design, launch tactics – all of that follows. Without loving and being wholly in what you do everything else will be superficial."

SCAN TO LISTEN

 MARK ASQUITH

Chapter Twelve
Razors and Blades.

Drew Vernon
Director of Education, USAtonies® USA, Salt Lake City, Utah, USA

"Our investment is focused on getting the tonies® box into homes, knowing it's just the beginning of a long customer journey."

Gaining Market Share in the American Toy Market

#ToniesUSA #ScreenFreePlay #EducationalToys #ChildDevelopment #DigitalDetox #USAmarket #EarlyLearning #InnovativeToys #MarketEntry #BrandGrowth

Introduction

In the competitive and dynamic world of tech toys, standing out is no small feat. Yet, tonies®, a company founded by Patric Faßbender and Marcus Stahl in Germany, has managed to do just that. With a mission to create a screen-free, imaginative, and educational experience for children, tonies® has grown into a €250 million business listed on the German Stock Exchange in Frankfurt. Drew Vernon, the Marketing Director for tonies® in America, shares his insights on how the company has achieved remarkable growth and brand recognition.

The Genesis of tonies®

The story of tonies® began in Germany in 2016 when Faßbender and Stahl, both fathers, observed their children's preschool teacher using a CD player to play songs and stories. Recognising the limitations of CDs, they envisioned a more durable, user-friendly, and independent play device for children. Thus, the toniebox was born – a five-inch speaker system encased in soft foam, designed to be durable and easy for children to use.

"The inspiration from these two dads was they actually met on the board of their children's preschool together. They saw their children's teacher using a CD player to play songs and stories. And they thought to themselves, CDs have been around since the eighties or the nineties. They scratch and they break. And most importantly, kids can't use them independently," explains Vernon.

Building Awareness in a New Market

When tonies® entered the American market, it faced the challenge of building brand awareness in a highly competitive category. Vernon emphasises the importance of telling people who they are and what they have to offer through various channels.

"First and foremost, we're trying to tell people who we are, what we have to offer. And we're trying to do that through a variety of different channels," says Vernon.

The Unique Selling Proposition

One of the key strategies for tonies® has been to highlight the unique features of their product. The toniebox uses RFID technology embedded in figurines called tonies®, which play different songs and stories when placed on the box. This screen-free, independent play device offers a refreshing alternative to the screen-dominated entertainment options available for children today.

"It's an independent play device. So a child can listen to the songs, listen to the stories in a screen-free way with or without adult supervision," Vernon notes.

Leveraging Media Relations

To get the product in front of consumers and the media, tonies® has focused on demonstrating the uniqueness and educational benefits of the toniebox. Vernon shares that winning awards and getting the product into the hands of publishers and editors has been a successful strategy.

"We've seen some success there in terms of winning awards. We won awards including Fast Company, 'Most Innovative Education Company,' and Good Housekeeping, 'Best Toys.' The Toy Association nominated us as a finalist for preschool toy of the year," Vernon shares.

The Role of Social Media

In today's digital age, social media is an indispensable tool for marketing. However, marketing a preschool toy presents unique challenges, as the consumers (children) and the customers (parents) are different people. Vernon explains the importance of demonstrating the benefits of the product to parents through platforms like Instagram, Facebook, and TikTok.

"When your consumer and your customer are different people, you need to give a consumer benefit to the customer, which is to say, mom, this is not just going to be a great device for your child, but it's actually going to be good for you because it's going to give you some time back in your day," Vernon explains.

Research and Validation

To substantiate the educational benefits of the toniebox, Vernon has commissioned research studies and engaged with thousands of teachers. The goal is to validate the positive impact of the toniebox on children's vocabulary, literacy, and even sleep patterns.

"I have commissioned a research study. It's basically set out to validate what I already know from talking to thousands of teachers for the last two years as part of our education initiative," Vernon states.

Distribution Strategy

Launching in the midst of a global shutdown in 2020, tonies® initially focused on building an online direct-to-consumer model. As the world reopened, they expanded into retail, including 700 independent specialty retailers and major chains like Target.

"We launched in 2020 in the middle of a shutdown that forced us to build primarily an online direct-to-consumer model. We got Amazon up pretty quickly as well, since that is a direct-to-consumer fulfilment," Vernon explains.

Investment and Growth

Vernon highlights the importance of investment in building a market from scratch. With the success in Germany as a backdrop, tonies® has the confidence to invest in the American market. The business model, which encourages repeat purchases of new figurines, ensures ongoing engagement with the product.

"The investment is in getting tonie® boxes into the hands of kids, because we know that that's going to be just the beginning for that family," Vernon notes.

Conclusion

In the competitive world of tech toys, tonies® has carved out a unique niche by offering a screen-free, educational, and imaginative play experience for children. Through strategic marketing, media relations, social media engagement, and a robust distribution strategy, tonies® has successfully built brand awareness and achieved significant growth.

As Vernon aptly puts it, "You need to find what that thing is for your business, what the significant need is that it solves, or find a new business."

The key take away for entrepreneurs is clear: identify a genuine need, create a unique solution, and communicate its benefits effectively to both consumers and customers. This approach not only helps in getting noticed but also ensures sustained growth and success.

SCAN TO LISTEN

 DREW VERNON

Chapter Thirteen
Digital Partnerships.

Ross Veitch
CEO & Co-Founder, Wego, Singapore

"A lot of travel brands went dark during COVID. They just disappeared. We trimmed around the edges, but we decided that we would keep the team intact. We're seeing market share gain."

Transforming Regional Travel Markets in Southeast Asia and the Middle East

#RossVeitch #Wego #OnlineTravel #MetaSearch #DigitalMarketing #TravelTech #SoutheastAsia #MiddleEastTravel #Entrepreneurship #COVID19Recovery

Introduction

In the international travel, tourism, and business centre of Asia, Singapore, Ross Veitch, co-founder of Wego, has built a billion-dollar travel enterprise. Alongside fellow Australian co-founder Craig Hewett, Veitch has navigated the complexities of the travel industry, transforming Wego into a leading online travel company in the Middle East and Southeast Asia.

The Genesis of Wego

Wego, an online travel company, operates on a dual-headquartered model with offices in Singapore and Dubai. Veitch explains, "We do a lot of our product tech data science work out of Singapore. We run the commercial marketing side of the business out of Dubai." This strategic division allows Wego to leverage the strengths of both locations, ensuring a robust operational framework.

Initially, Wego faced the classic cold start marketplace problem. "At its heart, Metasearch is a two-sided marketplace. On one side, you've got consumers looking to buy travel or search for travel, and on the other side, you've got merchants looking to sell travel," Veitch notes. To overcome this, Wego white-labelled their platform with major portals like Yahoo and MSN, effectively driving traffic and attracting merchants.

Navigating Market Challenges

Launching in 2005, Wego initially targeted Southeast Asia. However, the market was not ready. "Rather than sit around and wait for the market to develop, we looked further afield and realised there was a big untapped opportunity in the Middle East," Veitch recalls.

This pivot proved successful, with Wego becoming the biggest online travel app across the Middle East.

The COVID-19 pandemic posed another significant challenge. "In March 2020, everything came to a screaming halt," Veitch says. Despite a dramatic drop in revenue, Wego chose to maintain its team and double down on product development. "We kept the foot down on all the unpaid marketing channels. And that's paid off for us big time now," he adds.

Building the Brand

Wego's marketing strategy is a blend of performance-driven tactics and brand-building initiatives. "We think of ourselves as a primarily technology company that just happens to be operating in the travel industry," Veitch explains. This tech-centric approach is evident in their extensive use of digital marketing channels, including organic search optimisation, paid search, display marketing, PR, content marketing, and influencer marketing.

A significant portion of Wego's marketing budget is allocated to brand building. "We do TV, good old-fashioned TV. We try and do it in a fairly scientific, measured way," Veitch says. Partnering with the NBC group, Wego leverages the largest satellite TV network in the Gulf region to enhance brand visibility.

Content Marketing and Customer Engagement

Content marketing has been a cornerstone of Wego's strategy, particularly during the pandemic. "We made a decision, you know, when COVID hit to keep going with all of the unpaid channels," Veitch notes. This included a shift from inspirational content to practical information, helping travellers navigate the complex COVID-19 travel requirements.

Wego's blog has been particularly effective. "Our own blog has actually worked the hardest for us," Veitch reveals. By responding rapidly to trending travel topics and ensuring their content is picked up by Google News and other republishers, Wego has maintained a strong online presence.

Strategic Partnerships

Wego's success is also attributed to strategic partnerships with tourism boards, airlines, hotel chains, and mobile phone manufacturers. "We do a lot with Xiaomi and Samsung and Huawei. So we find ways to preload our app onto their phones," Veitch explains. These partnerships not only enhance Wego's visibility but also align the brand with other major players in the market.

Tourism boards play a crucial role in Wego's marketing efforts. "We typically put cash or cash and services into a pool and then we go out and market the destination together," Veitch says. This collaborative approach amplifies Wego's marketing budget and drives traffic to their platform.

The Role of AI in Future Growth

Looking ahead, Veitch emphasises the transformative potential of AI. "What's happening with AI now is going to be as big, if not bigger, than the creation of the internet," he asserts. For entrepreneurs, staying ahead of this technological curve is crucial. "If you're not already paying attention, I highly recommend you do," Veitch advises.

Conclusion

Wego provides a great case study in strategic brand building, courage, and adaptive marketing. The emphasis by Veitch on leveraging technology, maintaining robust partnerships, and staying agile in the face of market challenges provides a blueprint for entrepreneurs seeking to get their businesses noticed.

When it comes to facing the onslaught of AI, Veitch gives a veiled warning, "You want to be early. You really don't want to be late."

SCAN TO LISTEN

 # ROSS
VEITCH

Chapter Fourteen
Customer Experience.

Chris Schutrups
Founder, Managing Director, The Mortage Hut, Southampton, UK
Entrepreneur, Finance

*"Your job is to be the chief
storyteller of the business."*

#chrisschutrups #MortgageMastery #Entrepreneurship
#BusinessSuccess #BrandBuilding #LeadGeneration #SEO
#ContentMarketing #CustomerExperience #NicheMarketing

Introduction

In the competitive world of mortgage brokerage, standing out is no small feat. Chris Schutrups, founder and CEO of Mortgage Hut, based in Southampton, has managed to carve a niche for his company in a saturated market. From starting with a modest £10,000 loan from his parents to converting over 20,000 mortgage loans, Schutrups' journey offers invaluable lessons for entrepreneurs looking to get their businesses noticed.

The Early Days: Overcoming Initial Hurdles

Starting a business in the financial services sector comes with a unique set of challenges, particularly around cash flow and lead acquisition. Schutrups recalls, "If you come today, Jim, and you talk to me about a mortgage that you're looking to buy a new house somewhere, generally speaking, if we take an average, I don't see any income for up to nine months." This delay in revenue generation necessitated a strategic approach to scaling the business.

Initially, Schutrups relied on local estate agents for leads, a method that, while effective, came with its own set of challenges. "An estate agent may want somewhere between 25 and 40% of your gross income to give you that name and number," he explains. This significant cut into profits pushed Schutrups to explore more sustainable lead generation methods.

Building a Brand: The Importance of Consistency

One of the key strategies that Schutrups employed was consistency in marketing efforts. "At some point, we went from generating more leads off of our website than we did via our introduced business," he notes. This shift allowed Mortgage Hut to control its destiny better and improve the quality of leads.

Schutrups emphasises the importance of blending various marketing strategies. "We use different outreach. We obviously have a lot of data that we hold ourselves, about a hundred thousand subscribed potential customers that we'll market to," he says. This multifaceted approach ensures that the company is not overly reliant on a single source of leads, thereby mitigating risk.

Leveraging Technology: SEO and Content Marketing

In the digital age, SEO and content marketing have become indispensable tools for lead generation. Schutrups highlights, "The SEO is predominantly content led, you know, because we'll look at the longer tail search terms. We'll understand what people are searching for and create content based on that." This focus on content-driven SEO has allowed Mortgage Hut to attract a steady stream of organic leads.

Moreover, Schutrups is not afraid to experiment with new marketing techniques. "It's also about just going out there and trying things out, you know, testing and measuring and giving things a go," he advises. This willingness to innovate has been a cornerstone of Mortgage Hut's success.

Customer Engagement: Personal Touches Matter

One of the standout features of Mortgage Hut's customer engagement strategy is the personal touch that Schutrups himself brings to the table. "All of our customers get an email from me during the process and have the ability to reach out and speak to me directly," he shares. This direct line of communication not only builds trust but also ensures that customer concerns are addressed promptly.

Schutrups believes that a positive customer experience is paramount. "Our number one outcome that we're trying to achieve is an incredible customer experience," he asserts. This focus on customer satisfaction has led to high levels of customer loyalty and repeat business.

Niche Marketing: Targeting Specific Customer Segments

Mortgage Hut has also successfully employed niche marketing strategies to stand out in a crowded market. Schutrups explains, "We have two smaller brands, one being Police Mortgages, where we deal with 23 of the UK's police forces or federations and help police officers with their mortgages." By targeting specific customer segments with tailored solutions, Mortgage Hut has been able to build strong, loyal customer bases.

This approach extends to other niches as well. "We have another brand called Airline Mortgage Shop, where we deal with some of the UK's leading airlines in helping their staff get mortgages," he adds. By understanding the unique needs of these customer segments, Mortgage Hut can offer specialised services that larger, more generic brokers cannot.

Learning from Mistakes: The Facebook Marketing Lesson

Not all marketing strategies yield positive results, and Schutrups is candid about the lessons he has learned. In 2014, he discovered the power of Facebook marketing, which initially allowed him to scale his leads at a very low cost. However, as the platform became saturated with advertisers, the cost of acquiring customers skyrocketed. "It got to the point where I had two choices, because I had a load of advisors who were on salaries, and I had to pay their wages, but the leads that I was buying at the price I was buying, I was losing money," he recalls.

This experience taught Schutrups the importance of not becoming overly reliant on a single source of leads. "Plan as if those leads, either you can't afford them tomorrow or they're not there," he advises. This lesson in diversification has been crucial in ensuring the long-term sustainability of Mortgage Hut.

Conclusion

Chris Schutrups' experience of building the Mortgage Hut demonstrates the importance of understanding the value chain, niche marketing to maintain a personal touch with customers. He also recognises his role as the chief story teller of the business, and maintaining that vision over time.

"Once you get the right team, and you have that vision, and you have that dream, it's really important that your whole team understand where you're going and what you're trying to achieve."

"It's about trying to be consistent."

SCAN TO LISTEN

 CHRIS SCHUTRUPS

Chapter Fifteen
The Branded CEO.

Prateek Joshi

Investor at Moxxie Ventures | Author of 13 ML books |
Infinite ML podcast | ex Nvidia | AI Builder, CEO Plutoshift,
Palo Alto, California, USA

*"It becomes easy if you just do
one thing and keep doing it. The
compounding effect is amazing."*

Thought Leadership in the Machine Learning Industry

#PrateekJoshi #DualBrandingStrategy #MachineLearningInsights
#AIEntrepreneurship #BrandHumanization #CompoundingSuccess
#MLPhysicalWorld #InnovativeMLApplications #B2BSoftware
#EnterpriseAI

Introduction

Prateek Joshi, a machine learning engineer based in Palo Alto, California, has successfully built two distinct yet complementary brands: his corporate brand, PlutoShift, and his personal brand, Prateek Joshi. His story offers valuable lessons for entrepreneurs seeking to get their businesses noticed.

The Genesis of Two Brands

Prateek Joshi's career has been deeply rooted in machine learning. After studying the subject in school, he joined NVIDIA's machine learning team straight out of college. His passion for building practical products rather than focusing solely on research has been a consistent theme throughout his career. This drive led him to found PlutoShift, a company that leverages machine learning to address real-world problems, particularly in the physical world.

"Machine learning is becoming more ubiquitous in the cyber space or the virtual world, like search engines and e-commerce. But when it comes to the physical world, there's a pretty big gap," Joshi explains. This gap was the key motivation behind launching PlutoShift.

The Power of Focus

One of the key insights Joshi shares is the importance of focusing on a single area of expertise. "Once you find that one thing, it becomes easier to associate yourself with it," he says. By concentrating on machine learning, Joshi has been able to build a strong personal brand. "If you just do one thing and keep doing it, the compounding effect is amazing."

This focus has not only helped Joshi establish himself as a thought leader in machine learning but has also benefited PlutoShift. The company's brand is an extension of Joshi's professional expertise and his passion for climate issues. "The two brands that exist, they come from the same place, which is machine learning and climate," he notes.

The Importance of a Personal Brand

Joshi believes that having a personal brand is crucial for humanising a corporate entity. "PlutoShift, the company, it's an entity, right? It has a logo, but there's no face to it," he explains. By maintaining a personal brand, Joshi adds a human element to the company, making it more relatable and trustworthy.

"When you post something, when you write a book, when you write a blog post, when you talk, when you appear on podcasts, it puts a human face to it," he says. This authenticity is something that people appreciate and trust more than polished marketing messages from a corporate account.

Multi-Platform Presence

Joshi also emphasises the importance of being present on multiple platforms to reach a broader audience. "Different people consume content differently," he says. By having a personal website, a LinkedIn profile, and other social media accounts, Joshi ensures that he can connect with people in various ways.

"Once you have content with minimal extra work, you can use it for your website, your LinkedIn, or once you have an idea for a blog post, you can write the blog post, you can post the same on LinkedIn, you can convert that to short form content, you can talk about it," he explains. This strategy allows him to maximise the reach and impact of his content.

Engaging with Customers

Joshi's approach to customer engagement is another area where his personal brand plays a crucial role. "Initially, I just try to be helpful," he says. By offering free consultations and sharing his expertise, Joshi builds trust and establishes himself as a valuable resource.

"My goal is to reduce my electricity bills. That's my end goal. But I don't know how to connect this raw temperature data to that end goal," he explains. By helping potential customers understand how to achieve their goals, Joshi creates opportunities for PlutoShift to offer its products and services.

The Role of Thought Leadership

Joshi's personal brand also serves as a powerful tool for thought leadership. He frequently speaks at events, hosts a podcast, and writes extensively on topics related to machine learning and climate change. "I am doing all of that as Prateek Joshi," he says, noting that these activities are not directly tied to PlutoShift but help build his reputation and credibility.

Balancing Personal and Corporate Brands

Joshi is transparent with his employees and investors about the dual branding strategy. "I've been very open about this with our investors, our teammates, and potential future investors," he says. This openness has been well received and has even been a factor in attracting investors.

"Before they get attracted to the entity, they always look at the person first," he explains. By building a strong personal brand, Joshi enhances the credibility and attractiveness of PlutoShift. "Prateek Joshi as a brand can be used to accelerate, at least for the company, the top of the funnel."

Conclusion

Prateek Joshi's journey offers valuable lessons for entrepreneurs on the importance of building both personal and corporate brands. By focusing on a single area of expertise, maintaining a multi-platform presence, and engaging authentically with customers, Joshi has successfully built two complementary brands that enhance each other. The key take away is that a strong personal brand can humanise a corporate entity, build trust, and serve as a powerful tool for thought leadership and customer engagement.

SCAN TO LISTEN

 # PRATEEK JOSHI

Chapter Sixteen
Video Engagement.

Darin Dawson
Founder and CEO, BombBomb, Colorado Springs, Colorado, USA

"Video helps you build relationships and be face-to-face when you can't be face-to-face. Video helps you to personalise at scale."

#Darin Dawson #VideoCommunication #DigitalMarketing #Entrepreneurship #PersonalizedCommunication #BombBomb #TechInnovation #CustomerEngagement #MarketingStrategy #HumanizedCommunication

Introduction

In Colorado Springs, Colorado, nestled in the Rocky Mountains, Darin Dawson, co-founder of BombBomb, has been pioneering the use of video to help businesses communicate more effectively. With over 100,000 companies worldwide leveraging BombBomb's video solutions, Dawson foresaw the impact of video for mass communication and explains how he built a business on the trend of "being there when you can't be there."

Building Relationships Through Video

Dawson's journey with BombBomb began with a simple yet profound realisation: video can break through the noise and foster genuine connections. "When you're an entrepreneur, partnerships and relationships are so important," he explains. "Video helps you build relationships and be face-to-face when you can't be face-to-face."

The essence of BombBomb's approach is personalisation at scale. Dawson recounts his daily routine of sending personal video messages to introduce himself, express gratitude, or propose collaborations. This method, he asserts, is far more effective than traditional text-based communication. "People want to work with people they know, like, and trust," he says. "In this digital age, we get so much stuff thrown at us, but rarely do we have someone introduce themselves in a personal way."

Overcoming Psychological Barriers

Despite the clear advantages, many are hesitant to use video. Dawson identifies three primary psychological barriers: discomfort with one's voice, appearance, and uncertainty about what to say. "The way I hear my voice right now is not how you hear me," he notes. This discrepancy can make people uncomfortable with their recorded voice. Similarly, seeing oneself on camera can be unsettling, though this is becoming less of an issue with the rise of video conferencing tools like Zoom.

To overcome these barriers, Dawson advises entrepreneurs to embrace their authentic selves. "If you're an entrepreneur, you have the enthusiasm and passion for what you're doing. Bring that passion and enthusiasm through the video," he encourages. The key is to be brief, to the point, and genuine.

Practical Solutions with BombBomb

BombBomb addresses the practical challenges of video communication, such as file size and ease of use. "Our number one core competency is speed to video," Dawson states. BombBomb's platform allows users to quickly record and send videos, ensuring that they are easily received and viewed by the recipient. The platform also provides detailed feedback on engagement, such as whether the video was opened and how much of it was watched.

Moreover, BombBomb's focus on the recipient experience sets it apart. "We spend far more time on the recipient experience than on our user's experience," Dawson reveals. This approach ensures that the video is not only received but also engages the viewer effectively.

Enhancing Engagement and Response Rates

One of the standout features of BombBomb is its ability to provide a richer depth of engagement. Unlike traditional emails, video messages can convey tone, emotion, and personality, making them more compelling. "With video, I can tell you if they opened it, viewed it, and how much they viewed it," Dawson explains. This level of insight allows businesses to gauge the effectiveness of their communication and adjust accordingly.

BombBomb also offers a video page where recipients can interact with the video, leave comments, and engage with calls to action. This interactive element enhances the overall engagement and provides valuable feedback to the sender.

Seamless Integration and Branding

For businesses with larger teams or franchise networks, maintaining consistent branding is crucial. BombBomb's enterprise solutions allow for custom branding, ensuring that all videos align with the company's image. "We have email design templates and virtual backgrounds that can be controlled and locked down to just what the brand wants," Dawson says.

Additionally, BombBomb integrates seamlessly with various platforms, including Gmail, Outlook, Salesforce, and more. This flexibility ensures that users can incorporate video into their existing workflows without disruption.

Security and Compliance

In industries where security and compliance are paramount, BombBomb offers robust solutions. "We operate in financial services, mortgage transactions, real estate – these have to be secure and locked up," Dawson emphasises. BombBomb provides features such as message transcription, secure storage, and compliance monitoring, ensuring that all communications meet industry standards.

Building a Noteworthy Company

Beyond the technical aspects, Dawson attributes BombBomb's success to its strong team and commitment to customer service. "The team is so important as you're coming up," he reflects. "You can't do it by yourself; you need help." BombBomb's culture, built on values of humility, service, flexibility, and relationships, has been instrumental in creating a positive work environment and fostering loyalty among employees and customers alike.

Dawson also highlights the importance of being a reliable partner. "I want to do what I say I'm going to do. I'm going to come through for my partners and my customers," he asserts. This dedication to customer satisfaction has helped BombBomb build a reputation for excellence and reliability.

Conclusion

Darin Dawson's insights underscore the transformative power of video in modern marketing. By leveraging video to build genuine connections, overcoming psychological barriers, and ensuring seamless integration and security, entrepreneurs can significantly enhance their communication strategies.

As Dawson aptly puts it, "People want to work with people they know, like, and trust."

Embracing video can help businesses achieve this goal, fostering deeper engagement and driving success.

SCAN TO LISTEN

 ## DARIN DAWSON

Chapter Seventeen
NFT Rewards.

Ed Vincent

Tech Founder | Entertainment CEO | Capital Factory Portfolio Company | Advisor | Data & Growth Expert | AI & Web3 Evangelist | First Ever Lifetime Live Event Pass, Festival Pass, Austin, Texas, USA

"By creating the NFT and creating this lifetime value, the perceived value is very great for people."

Pioneering Event Attendance with NFT-Based Subscriptions

#EdVincent #FestivalPass #NFTCommunity #EventTech #ExperientialMarketing #DigitalToken #LiveEvents #BlockchainTechnology #InnovativeEntrepreneurship #AustinStartups

Introduction

Leveraging Non-Fungible Tokens (NFTs) and Experiential Marketing: Insights from Ed Vincent of Festival Pass

Ed Vincent, an entrepreneur based in Austin, Texas, shared his extensive experience and innovative strategies in the events and entertainment industry. Vincent, the founder of Festival Pass, has a rich history of building and exiting multiple businesses over the past 25 years. His latest venture, Festival Pass, is a unique platform that leverages NFTs to create lifetime memberships for live events and hotels. Here, we distil the essence of Vincent's insights on marketing, brand building, and customer engagement.

The Power of NFTs in Membership Models

Vincent's latest project, Festival Pass, utilises NFTs to offer a lifetime membership model. This approach not only provides significant value to customers but also ensures long-term engagement with the brand. "If you buy and own an NFT, you get a lifetime membership to our platform," Vincent explains. "Once you buy it once and pay for it once, you get $1,200 worth of credits on our platform to be able to use for live events and hotels anywhere you want."

This innovative use of NFTs helps overcome anxieties around new technology by simplifying the concept. "It's something unique to us, and it's something that if you own it, you get benefits. It's that simple," Vincent adds. By limiting the number of NFTs to 10,000, Festival Pass creates a sense of exclusivity and loyalty among its members.

Experiential Marketing: Bringing Brands to Life

Vincent's background in experiential marketing has significantly influenced his approach to brand building. Experiential marketing involves creating live, interactive experiences that engage consumers directly with the brand. "All it actually means is taking your brand and doing something with it live in market," Vincent clarifies. "Whether you're showing up to an event and having a branded bar or bringing a car to a mall and doing a sweepstakes around that car, it's about physical activity where the consumer is experiencing something in real life with your brand."

One of the standout strategies Vincent employs is the creation of a digital content studio within a bus, in partnership with Spin Magazine. This mobile studio allows Festival Pass to produce high-quality content on the go, interviewing rock stars and other celebrities at major events like South by Southwest. "We've wrapped it on the outside with Spin and Festival Pass branding, so the entire 40-foot bus is a huge billboard going through Austin, Texas," Vincent notes. This approach not only generates content but also serves as a moving advertisement, enhancing brand visibility.

Influencer Partnerships: A Symbiotic Relationship

In the realm of live events, influencers play a crucial role in driving attendance and engagement. Vincent has effectively leveraged influencer partnerships by offering them free tickets to events in exchange for promotion. "We've offered to a bunch of influencers that, as long as you talk about our product, we'll give you some free tickets to some events," Vincent says. This mutually beneficial arrangement allows influencers to create content while promoting Festival Pass, thereby reaching a wider audience.

Vincent provides a practical example: "We're going to have a lot of influencers that all want to go to Coachella, and they're going to talk about our lifetime membership. They'll say, 'I was looking for my ticket to Coachella and stumbled across this thing called Festival Pass. If you buy their lifetime membership, you get your ticket to Coachella this year, and then every year for the rest of your life, you get a free ticket to Coachella.'"

Starting Local to Grow Global

One of the key lessons Vincent has learned over his entrepreneurial journey is the importance of starting local before expanding globally. "Sometimes when people launch something, they think it's easier to let everybody get to it, whether that's nationally or globally," Vincent observes. "But usually, the best way to launch any brand, especially from a cost-effective standpoint, is to go deep with a specific geography, audience, or vertical."

Festival Pass initially launched nationally, but Vincent soon realised the value of concentrating efforts locally. "We're doubling down now on local," he says. "The content studio bus will help us have a massive presence locally. If it works, we'll take that experience elsewhere."

Conclusion

Ed Vincent's insights offer valuable lessons for entrepreneurs in the events and entertainment industry. By leveraging NFTs for membership models, employing experiential marketing, forming strategic influencer partnerships, and focusing on local markets before expanding globally, businesses can effectively build their brand and engage customers.

"More word of mouth, something that goes deeper into a certain vertical, just works better. It always gets more traction."

SCAN TO LISTEN

 ED
VINCENT

Chapter Eighteen
Consistency Wins.

Eric L. Schmidt
Co-Founder and CEO, Glue Up, Washington, DC, USA

"In B2B, I think it's really about consistency and over time, that consistency then builds the brand, then builds your customer base to be able to look at you in a different way."

Building a Global App to Serve Community-Based Organisations

#GlueUp #SaaSI #GlobalBusiness #MembershipManagement #Entrepreneurship #MarketExpansion #DigitalInnovation #B2BSoftware #CRM #CommunityBuilding

Building a Global Brand: Insights from Eric Schmidt of Glue Up

In the B2B space, getting noticed is a long game. While consumer marketing is about meeting short-term personal wants, business marketing is aimed at solving long-term organisational needs. Eric Schmidt, co-founder of Glue Up, a community engagement customer relationship management (CRM) solution based in McLean, Virginia, has navigated this terrain with remarkable success. Celebrating the 10th anniversary of his company, Schmidt shares invaluable insights into marketing, brand building, and customer engagement, particularly when marketing to B2B customers.

The Evolution of Glue Up

Originally known as EventBank, founded in 2013, Glue Up has transformed from a small husband-and-wife team into a global operation with 110 employees and 12 offices worldwide. The company serves over 1,200 clients, primarily in the chamber of commerce and association space. Schmidt explains, "Glue Up is what we consider a community engagement CRM solution. We provide a full suite of what we call all-in-one solutions to our customers."

The rebranding from EventBank to Glue Up was a strategic move to better reflect the company's expanded capabilities beyond event management. "We realised that our name was limiting our ability to convince people that we weren't just about events," Schmidt notes. "We were bringing people together through our technology, and our name was not conveying that message."

Navigating Global Markets

Expanding into the global market posed unique challenges, particularly in understanding the diverse needs of different regions. "The needs of somebody in Asia are different than those in Africa and very different from those in the United States," Schmidt observes. This required a product that could be adapted to various markets, a task that took considerable time and effort.

One of the key lessons Schmidt learned was the importance of mobile technology, especially in regions like Asia and Africa. "We had to learn early on how to really make sure that we could build for mobile," he says. This focus on mobile technology proved prescient, especially during the COVID-19 pandemic when remote work became the norm.

Marketing Strategies and Challenges

Marketing a software product globally is no small feat. Schmidt shares that one of the most significant challenges was LinkedIn marketing. "We spent a lot of money on LinkedIn marketing, which is very expensive compared to other platforms, and we just did not see the ROI from it," he admits. This experience underscored the importance of understanding where your customers are and how best to reach them.

Consistency in marketing efforts has been crucial for Glue Up. "In B2B, I think it's really about consistency. Over time, that consistency then builds the brand and your customer base," Schmidt explains. This approach has helped Glue Up build trust with its clients, a critical factor in the B2B space.

Customer Engagement in the Digital Age

The COVID-19 pandemic forced many organisations to rethink their approach to events and customer engagement. Glue Up responded by developing new tools like Speed Networking to facilitate virtual interactions. "Our speed networking tool was really built from some of those events that we were all attending, whether it was a happy hour or just a gathering of people at a restaurant," Schmidt says.

These tools have proven invaluable for distributed workforces, helping teams build relationships and maintain a sense of community even when working remotely. "Our team members in the United States were meeting people in Hong Kong, our team members in the Philippines were meeting folks in South Africa," Schmidt shares. This global connectivity is essential for any growing business.

Lessons Learned and Future Directions

Reflecting on the past decade, Schmidt acknowledges that there have been many lessons learned along the way. One of the most important is the need for continuous improvement and adaptation. "A software is never done. There's always something another customer would like to see," he notes.

Looking ahead, Schmidt is focused on continuing to empower organisations worldwide with Glue Up's technology. "We still have a long way to go, but we're committed to achieving our mission and really empowering these organisations worldwide," he says.

Conclusion

Eric Schmidt's journey with Glue Up offers valuable lessons for entrepreneurs seeking to get their businesses noticed. From the importance of consistency in marketing to the need for adaptability in a global market, Schmidt's insights are a testament to the power of perseverance and innovation. As he aptly puts it, "In B2B, it's really about trust and consistently showing up over time, building and learning, but staying in the long game."

SCAN TO LISTEN

 ## ERIC SCHMIDT

Chapter Nineteen
Lumpy Marketing.

Brad Sugars
Founder, ActionCOACH, Las Vegas, Nevada, USA

"People do not buy a franchise; they join a team. They are joining a movement."

Building a Profitable Global Coaching Franchise

#BradSugars #ActionCOACH #Entrepreneurship #BusinessCoaching #Franchising #PublicSpeaking #StrategicPartnerships #Leadership #MarketingStrategy #BusinessGrowth

Introduction

Brad Sugars, the founder and CEO of ActionCOACH, has built an impressive franchise business with over 1,100 offices worldwide. Originally from Australia, now based in Las Vegas, Nevada, Sugars has authored over 16 books and is recognised as one of the world's top coaches. In this article, he shares invaluable insights into how he has successfully built and maintained his brand, offering actionable advice for entrepreneurs seeking to get their businesses noticed.

Recruiting the Best Talent

One of the cornerstones of Sugars' strategy is recruiting top-tier talent. He emphasises the importance of not just hiring but actively recruiting individuals who can add significant value to the team. "I always recruited the best of the best. I would never try and recruit people to my team that I didn't think would add value to the team in a massive way," he explains. This proactive approach to building a team ensures that the business is always moving forward with the right people in place.

Embracing Public Speaking and Partnerships

Sugars has never shied away from the stage, understanding the power of visibility. "In the early days, I did more than 200 events in a year. So, I was on stage everywhere," he recalls. This relentless pursuit of public speaking opportunities helped him build a strong personal and business brand.

Partnerships have also played a crucial role in his strategy. Sugars partnered with newspaper groups, magazines, radio stations, and chambers of commerce, often offering his services for free to gain exposure. "In those first two years, just the newspaper group in Australia put me in front of 288,000 business owners," he notes. These partnerships allowed him to reach a massive audience and establish his brand.

Innovative Marketing Techniques

Sugars is a master of innovative marketing techniques, particularly when it comes to getting his foot in the door. He shares a memorable strategy involving lumpy mail: "I bought the right arm off a bunch of mannequins... and we'd send this in a box to you. It said, 'I'd give my right arm for an hour of your time.'" This creative approach ensured that his messages stood out and captured the recipient's attention.

He also used direct mail campaigns with unique twists, such as sending invitations on a silver platter or attaching a band-aid to an envelope with the message, "Stop the band-aid solutions to your business." These tactics not only got him noticed but also demonstrated his commitment to thinking outside the box.

Building a Franchise Network

Building a successful franchise network requires more than just a good business model; it requires a compelling vision and a strong sense of community. "People don't buy a franchise; they join a team," Sugars asserts. He emphasises the importance of having a clear vision and culture that potential franchisees can buy into.

Marketing also plays a significant role in attracting franchisees. Sugars highlights the importance of being everywhere and doing everything to get noticed. "You've got to do great marketing. You've got to be everywhere," he advises. This omnipresent approach ensures that the brand remains top-of-mind for potential franchisees.

The Power of Community and Accountability

Sugars believes that the success of a franchise lies in the support and community it offers. "We believe franchisees and our customers come to us for four things: community, accountability, results, and education," he explains. By fostering a strong community and providing ongoing education and accountability, ActionCOACH ensures that its franchisees are well equipped to succeed.

Balancing Multiple Brands

Managing multiple brands can be challenging, but Sugars has found a way to balance his personal brand with the ActionCOACH brand. "The Brad Sugars brand can go and do things on the way. If you look at someone, you know, I'm nowhere near as famous, but an Elon Musk, the Tesla brand is here. The SpaceX brand is here. The Elon Musk brand is here," he elaborates. By maintaining distinct brand promises for each, Sugars can cater to different audiences and market segments effectively.

Conclusion

Brad Sugars' approach to marketing and brand building offers a masterclass in getting noticed. From recruiting top talent, partnerships, prolific public speaking schedules, to innovative marketing techniques and building a strong community, his strategies are both practical and inspiring.

"Your business cannot outgrow you. The more you learn, the more you earn. And as the owner of a business, if you stop learning, then your business is going to stop growing."

SCAN TO LISTEN

 BRAD SUGARS

Chapter Twenty
Need for Speed.

Jonathan Rosenfeld
Rosenfeld Injury Lawyers LLC, Chicago, Illinois, USA

"Speed is key. We've found that responding within a couple of minutes drastically increases our rate of signing a case compared to waiting overnight."

Understanding the Emergency of an Emergency to Win Legal Clients

#RosenfeldInjuryLawyers #PersonalInjuryLaw #LegalMarketing #ContentStrategy #ClientService #BrandBuilding #DigitalMarketing #LawFirmGrowth #StrategicInnovation #ClientEngagement

Introduction

From the windy city of Chicago, Jonathan Rosenfeld has built a healthy business in the highly competitive field of personal injury law. His practice, Rosenfeld Injury Lawyers, has recovered over $250 million for clients and currently manages over 4,000 active files. Rosenfeld's success is not merely a result of legal acumen but a testament to his innovative marketing strategies and relentless pursuit of brand building.

The Power of Content Creation

Rosenfeld attributes much of his success to a robust content creation strategy. Unlike traditional marketing, which often focuses on direct selling, Rosenfeld emphasises the importance of educational content. "I'm talking about creating content that actually solves a problem or answers a question for a prospective client," he explains.

In today's digital age, potential clients are more informed than ever. By the time they reach out, they have often conducted extensive research. Rosenfeld's approach is to provide comprehensive information on various aspects of personal injury law, from insurance queries to case valuations. "People may not remember the person who just tries selling them everything. But at the end of the day, what I hear consistently is, 'I just had to call you. I kept seeing your information, every search I was doing on whatever it was.'"

Speed and Accessibility

In the realm of personal injury law, speed is of the essence. Clients often contact lawyers in a state of distress, requiring immediate assistance. Rosenfeld's firm is available 24/7, ensuring that no query goes unanswered. "If we respond within a couple of minutes, our rate of signing the case increases drastically," he notes.

To facilitate this, Rosenfeld Injury Lawyers employs a team of intake specialists who handle live calls around the clock. Additionally, the firm offers multiple contact methods, including phone, text, and live chat, to cater to the varying preferences of potential clients. "We try to tailor our services to really what people want and need," Rosenfeld says.

Leveraging Technology

Managing a high volume of enquiries requires a sophisticated system. Rosenfeld's firm uses Captura, a legal platform that integrates with their case management system. This allows them to track every interaction, ensuring consistency and efficiency. "I love having data. I love having that ability to track things. And it's really crucial as a business owner to track where your business is coming from," he explains.

The Role of Video and Multimedia

In an era where consumers expect rich, multimedia experiences, Rosenfeld has embraced video content. His website features YouTube videos where he discusses various aspects of personal injury law. "People today expect to see video. They expect to see graphics. They expect everything," he asserts.

While not every visitor will engage with every piece of content, the combination of text, video, and graphics builds trust and credibility. "It's sort of the combination of those things, which really helps. It builds trust with your prospective client," Rosenfeld adds.

Consistency and Persistence

One of the most valuable lessons Rosenfeld offers is the importance of consistency. Building a brand and establishing a strong online presence is not an overnight endeavour. "Be consistent and just keep going," he advises. Many business owners give up too soon, disheartened by the lack of immediate results. However, Rosenfeld emphasises that success often comes from "the constant tinkering, the constant grinding."

Referral Networks

Given the volume of cases his firm handles, Rosenfeld has developed a robust referral network. In the USA, personal injury lawyers can refer cases to other attorneys and receive referral fees. This system allows Rosenfeld to ensure that clients receive the best possible representation, even if it means referring them to another lawyer. "It's a win-win situation for everyone," he says. "My success is dependent on the reputation I have and the success I have with the client."

Conclusion

Rosenfeld's approach to marketing and brand building offers valuable lessons for entrepreneurs. By focusing on educational content, ensuring rapid response times, leveraging technology, and maintaining consistency, businesses can build trust and attract clients.

Rosenfeld provides this encouragement. "Just keep going, be persistent, and good things will happen." This relentless commitment to providing value and building trust, even during the hard times, is the best insurance available to protect a brand from injury.

SCAN TO LISTEN

 JONATHAN ROSENFELD

Chapter Twenty-One
Amplifier Effect.

Mona Akmal
CEO and founder of FalkonAI, Seattle, Washington, USA

"We are transitioning from human-led revenue generation to insight-led revenue generation, and it requires marketing, sales, and customer success to all come together."

Introducing Augmented Analytics to a Market Trying to Understand It

#MonaAkmal #FalkonAI #Entrepreneurship #SoftwareMarketing #CustomerEngagement #ProductLedGrowth #Innovation #StartupFunding #IntegratedMarketing #TechnologyAdoption

Introduction

Mona Akmal, originally from Pakistan, has carved a remarkable path from being a project manager at Microsoft to founding Falcon AI, a company based in Seattle. With over $20 million raised in funding, Akmal's journey is a testament to the power of vision, persistence, and strategic marketing. In a recent conversation, she shared invaluable insights into how she has managed to get her business noticed in a crowded market.

The Genesis of Falcon AI

Falcon AI addresses a critical gap in the market by unifying data across marketing, sales, and customer success teams to generate actionable insights. Akmal explains, "Modern selling does not work the way it used to. Increasingly, we are giving away our products and services for free, so all of our revenue is a function of expansion." This shift from human-led to insight-led revenue generation is at the core of Falcon AI's value proposition.

Overcoming the Status Quo

One of the most significant challenges Falcon AI faces is overcoming the status quo. Akmal likens it to "selling to a lion that has had a thorn stuck in its paw for 10 years." The key, she says, is to help people understand the pain they've lived with and how Falcon AI can alleviate it. "It's only when the market dynamic shifts that change becomes possible," she notes, highlighting the rise of product-led growth and usage-based pricing as catalysts for this shift.

Building a Market Through Early Adopters

Akmal's strategy for market penetration involves targeting early adopters. "We don't need every customer out there to be a visionary, but we need our first 20 customers to be people who already see where the puck is going," she explains. By identifying and engaging with strategic modern revenue leaders in micro-communities, Falcon AI has been able to build a strong foundation.

Leveraging LinkedIn for Customer Engagement

LinkedIn has been a crucial platform for Falcon AI's customer engagement strategy. Akmal describes the process: "It starts with just following them and then starting a conversation, probably simply through a comment or sharing an opinion on something that they've posted." This approach not only builds relationships but also helps identify other valuable communities. "It's more about seeking those people out online, building relationships with them, and then learning through them where other people like them are," she adds.

Amplifying Reach Through Influencers

To scale their reach, Falcon AI employs a multi-pronged strategy involving social influencers. "We have 100 social influencers who are working with us, and each one of them has 10 to 100,000 followers that are our target market," Akmal reveals. This approach allows Falcon AI to access a million of the most relevant people through a network of micro-influencers.

The Role of Public Relations and Content

Public relations (PR) and high-value content are also integral to Falcon AI's brand-building efforts. "We work with a phenomenal PR agency that is helping me get out there and have conversations to talk about issues that are pertinent to Falcon and Falcon's customers," Akmal says. Additionally, the company focuses on developing bite-sized, shareable content and is even exploring platforms like TikTok to reach a broader audience.

Raising Capital as a First-Time Founder

Raising $20 million as a first-time founder is no small feat, especially for someone who doesn't fit the typical tech founder stereotype. Akmal attributes her success to a decade-long journey of becoming a known entity in the startup world. "I decided to become a known entity. I put myself through CEO school, working for three very different CEOs building three very different companies," she shares. This experience allowed her to build relationships with investors and become a trusted figure in the startup community.

Transitioning to a Leadership Role

As Falcon AI grows, Akmal is transitioning from direct ownership to leading through people. "We use OKRs (Objectives and Key Results) to set objectives for the company. It is my job to set those objectives, no more than three, and then every leader at the company is responsible for defining key results," she explains. This structured approach ensures that everyone is aligned and accountable for the company's success.

Simplifying Internal Communications

Despite the complexity of Falcon AI's operations, Akmal prefers to keep internal communications simple. "We use the simplest common tool that everyone knows how to use, which is a Google spreadsheet," she says. This approach allows different teams to use their preferred productivity tools while maintaining a unified system for tracking company-level objectives.

Conclusion

Mona Akmal's journey from Microsoft to Falcon AI offers a masterclass in strategic marketing and leadership. Her emphasis on early adopters, leveraging LinkedIn, and employing a multi-pronged influencer strategy provides actionable insights for entrepreneurs.

"For the first five years of your company's life, people are buying you as much as they're buying your software." This focus on personal and brand alignment is crucial for getting noticed in today's competitive market.

SCAN TO LISTEN

 MONA AKMAL

Chapter Twenty-Two
Customer Stories.

Aron Clymer
Formerly Founder and CEO of Data Clymer, Partner | Data Solutions, Spaulding Ridge, Minneapolis, Minnesota, USA

"Every step felt like we were building not just a business, but a community – a network of clients, partners, and a dedicated team."

Introducing Data Analytics Through Partnerships

#DataClymer #AronClymer #DataServices #Entrepreneurship
#BusinessStrategy #ProfessionalServices #StartupGrowth
#DataSystems #BusinessDevelopment #StrategicPartnerships

Introduction

In the heart of Minneapolis, Minnesota, often referred to as the "City of Lakes," Aaron Clymer has carved out a niche in the data services industry. As the founder and CEO of DataClymer, Aaron successfully navigated the challenging waters of entrepreneurship, growing his company from a startup to a 50-person enterprise in less than six years.

Building DataClymer: From Concept to Reality

Aaron's journey began with a solid foundation in corporate America, where he spent 15–20 years honing his skills in management, team building, and data systems. This experience proved invaluable when he decided to take the plunge into entrepreneurship. "I always think in retrospect, I wish I'd done it even earlier, but at the same time, my experience really helped," Aaron reflects.

DataClymer, a professional services firm specialising in data systems and data warehouses, primarily serves mid-sized clients. Aaron's transition from a corporate role to founding DataClymer was facilitated by leveraging existing relationships. "I went and talked to a vendor that I already had worked with as part of my corporate job… within three weeks, I actually had my first client," he recalls.

Overcoming Initial Challenges

One of the significant challenges Aaron faced was balancing capacity with demand, especially since he bootstrapped the entire venture. "I didn't want to get in over my skis too much and land a client that was too large because I didn't have the team to support it," he explains. This delicate balance required careful client selection and strategic growth.

Aaron also emphasised the importance of partnerships in generating business. "All of my leads were coming through my partners... I kind of had to just take whatever I was given and make it work," he notes. This reliance on partners necessitated a proactive approach to maintaining those relationships.

Leveraging Partnerships for Growth

Aaron's strategy for keeping his brand top of mind with partners, particularly Salesforce, was crucial. "I would call my partners and see if I could speak at their quarterly business review or their annual meeting," he says. By sharing joint customer stories and maintaining visibility, Aaron ensured that DataClymer remained a go-to resource for his partners' clients.

Interestingly, Aaron found that maintaining his own brand identity was generally more beneficial than operating under a partner's umbrella. "In almost all cases, we were able to keep our own brand and simply be a partner," he explains. This approach allowed DataClymer to build its brand while benefiting from partner relationships.

Scaling the Business

As DataClymer grew, Aaron recognised the need to delegate and transition his role. "The trick was at some point realising, okay, delegation is the key. I have to delegate everything," he admits. This shift allowed him to focus on strategic thinking and being the face of the company.

Hiring a full-time marketing and sales team was a pivotal move. "It's really just been this year when I finally transitioned into fully delegating everything away from myself and being more of the face of the company," Aaron shares. This transition was essential for scaling the business and maintaining growth.

Marketing Strategies and Lessons Learned

Aaron's marketing journey involved a mix of in-house efforts and external agencies. Initially, he tried using an external firm for LinkedIn marketing, but the results were mixed. "We did get meetings, but not very much conversion on those meetings," he notes. This experience led him to favour in-house marketing efforts, which proved more effective.

Investing in a full-time marketing team had a significant impact on brand awareness. "When we started the journey, before I had hired these teams, we only had about 300 LinkedIn followers... Fast forward to nine months later, we're over a thousand followers," Aaron proudly states. This increase in brand visibility was achieved through consistent content creation, webinars, eBooks, and active engagement on LinkedIn.

The Importance of Failing Fast and Persevering

One of the key lessons Aaron shares is the importance of failing fast and persevering. "Fail fast in everything you do, especially in marketing... You will figure it out," he advises. This mindset, coupled with opportunistic hiring and strategic investments, has been instrumental in DataClymer's success.

Conclusion

Aaron Clymer's journey with DataClymer offers valuable insights for entrepreneurs seeking to get their businesses noticed. From leveraging partnerships and maintaining brand identity to investing in marketing and embracing a fail-fast mentality, Aaron's strategies provide a roadmap for success.

As he aptly puts it, "Expanding your network, talking to other entrepreneurs… you just learn so much." This approach has not only helped Aaron build a successful business but also navigate the complexities of scaling and brand building.

Postscript

DataClymer was acquired by Spaulding Ridge, an award-winning business transformation firm, in April 2024. I decided to retain the story because the acquisition demonstrates the success of Clymer's strategy.

SCAN TO LISTEN

 ARON CLYMER

Chapter Twenty-Three
Advance Marketing.

Emeric Ernoult
Founder and CEO, Agorapulse, Paris, France

"I built a system to let people know about how great my product would be, before my product was actually great."

Helping Companies to See the Value in Their Social Media

#Agorapulse #EmericErnoult #SocialMediaManagement
#DigitalMarketing #Entrepreneurship #BusinessGrowth
#SocialMediaTools #MarketingStrategy #ClientEngagement
#InnovationInBusiness #France

Introduction

In the French capital Paris, Emeric Ernoult, CEO and founder of Agorapulse, has been bringing order to the way businesses manage their social media presence. For entrepreneurs grappling with the chaos of multiple social media channels, Ernoult's journey from a bootstrapped startup to a $24 million revenue company offers invaluable lessons.

The Problem of Social Media Overwhelm

Ernoult identified a common pain point for businesses: the overwhelming task of managing multiple social media platforms. "It's a bit overwhelming. It's all over the place. You have to log in, log out in many different platforms, many different places," he explains. Agorapulse was born out of this need to streamline social media management, providing a centralised solution that not only schedules content but also measures its impact.

Measuring Return on Investment: The Secret Sauce

One of Agorapulse's standout features is its ability to measure the return on investment (ROI) from social media activities. "We are able to look at conversion and revenue, platform by platform, profile by profile, content, piece of content by piece of content, member by team member," says Ernoult. This granular approach allows businesses to see the direct impact of their social media efforts, a feature so unique that Ernoult has filed a patent for it in the USA.

Practical Application: Tracking Content Through the Funnel

Ernoult's approach to tracking social media content is both innovative and practical. By adapting existing technologies used in email marketing and paid advertising, Agorapulse can track the performance of organic social media content. "We took those principles and those technologies and applied them to organic social," he notes. This allows businesses to see which specific actions on social media are driving value, providing a clear picture of what works and what doesn't.

Success Stories: Small Businesses Leading the Way

Interestingly, it's often the smaller businesses that excel in generating revenue through social media. Ernoult shares the story of a small business selling plant-based medicine, which generates approximately $75,000 a month on Instagram alone. "Small businesses are more flexible in trying social as a channel, as a way to grow their business," he observes. This flexibility allows them to leverage social media more effectively, often outperforming larger companies.

Common Mistakes in Social Media Marketing

Ernoult highlights two common mistakes businesses make with social media. The first is treating social media merely as a distribution channel for content. "You have to find a way to make your social content engaging," he advises. Simply posting links and titles won't capture the audience's interest. Instead, businesses should aim to trigger conversations and engage with their audience.

The second mistake is prioritising social media when it may not be the right channel for their business at that time. "In my early days, I focused on SEO content and influencers. I didn't do anything on social for at least 2–3 years until 3–4 million of revenue," Ernoult recalls. Understanding when and how to invest in social media is crucial for long-term success.

Building Agorapulse: A Journey of Continuous Learning

Ernoult's journey with Agorapulse is a testament to the importance of continuous learning and adaptation. "As a business owner, you are not the right person to take your business to the next step. You have to become that person," he asserts. This involves surrounding oneself with knowledgeable peers, mentors, and constantly investing in personal development.

Transitioning Strategies: From Small- and Medium-Sized Business Inbound to Mid-Market Outbound

As Agorapulse grew, so did its marketing strategy. Initially focused on small- and medium-sized businesses (SMBs) through inbound marketing, the company has now shifted towards targeting mid-market clients through outbound efforts. "We had to move from SMB inbound to more mid-market outbound," Ernoult explains. This involves proactively identifying and reaching out to ideal customers, rather than relying solely on inbound traffic.

The Importance of Laying Groundwork

One of the key strategies Ernoult employed was building a system to drive traffic to Agorapulse's website before the product was fully ready. "I had to build a system to let people know about how great my product is before my product is actually great," he says. This long-term view ensured that when the product was ready, the audience was already there.

Conclusion

The dynamic rise of Agorapulse can be attributed to the advance "seeding" of the product with influencers. Ernoult was engaged with customers and showed them how they could start measuring ROI for their social media work. In the process, he has had to also grow as a person, to lead the ever larger business.

Ernoult encourages entrepreneurs with the message, "You have to become the person who can take your business to the next step."

SCAN TO LISTEN

 EMERIC
ARNOULT

Chapter Twenty-Four
Persistence and Perfection.

Gail Kasper

Two-Time TEDx Speaker, World Class Speaker in Customised Sales Programs, Philadelphia, USA

"It's always to me about elevating your brand, elevate it, elevate it."

Building Self-Belief

#GailKasper #Entrepreneurship #PersonalBrand
#ProfessionalSpeaking #MediaPresence #CoachingSuccess
#SocialMediaStrategy #Philadelphia #Resilience #StrategicInnovation

Introduction

In Philadelphia, also known as Philly, Pennsylvania, Gail Kasper has carved out a niche for herself as a TV celebrity, professional coach, and trainer. With a social media following exceeding 300,000, two published books, and 10 audiobooks, Kasper has become a beacon for entrepreneurs seeking to get their businesses noticed. Her journey, marked by resilience and strategic thinking, offers invaluable lessons in brand building, social media engagement, and media relations.

The Journey to Becoming a Media Celebrity

Gail Kasper's path to success was not straightforward. Initially uncertain about her career direction, she found herself working for various companies before discovering her passion for professional speaking. "I was a manager and a bad manager," she admits, 'but I learned a lot about leadership and how to build a team." This realisation led her to pursue a career in professional speaking, a decision that would eventually propel her into the limelight.

Kasper's first significant challenge came when she was unexpectedly fired from a training organisation after landing a TV show. "I found myself overnight on my own, in my own business," she recalls. With no money in the bank and no resources, she hit the pavement, leveraging her network to secure her first client. "It was all about hitting the pavement, talking to people that I knew," she says. This initial effort led to a cascade of opportunities, eventually allowing her to train up and down the East Coast for ADT Security Services.

Building a Brand from Scratch

One of the most compelling aspects of Kasper's story is her ability to build a brand from the ground up. Her first client came through a personal connection at ADT, who offered her a small contract. "It was within his realm to say, okay, we've got a budget for $400," she explains. This small opportunity was the seed that grew into a flourishing business.

Kasper emphasises the importance of networking and humility in the early stages of building a brand. "Go back to the place where you began, go back to the place where you had nothing," she advises. Attending networking events, Chamber of Commerce meetings, and Rotary clubs can be invaluable for making connections and getting your name out there.

Leveraging Media Opportunities

Kasper's transition from a $400 contract to becoming a media celebrity is a testament to her persistence and resilience. She initially aspired to be a newscaster and even had a scholarship to Temple University, but she dropped out after two years. "My first semester was really tough in the communications world," she says. However, her dream of being on TV never faded.

Her big break came when she met with America's TV Job Network, a TV show looking for hosts. Despite having no experience, she persisted for three months, showing up every day until she was finally given a chance. "I went to the audition and I got the job," she says. This opportunity opened the door to numerous other media engagements, including her own TV show, Gail Kasper TV.

The Power of Resilience and Self-Belief

Kasper's story is a powerful example of the importance of resilience and self-belief in overcoming obstacles. "Make a fool of yourself," she advises. "It's that resilience inside yourself." Her persistence paid off, allowing her to build a substantial following and a strong personal brand.

Even now, Kasper continues to face new challenges and opportunities with the same tenacity. "Every day of my life, you're faced with a new opportunity or something new that you want to do," she says. Her ability to push through self-doubt and keep moving forward is a key factor in her success.

Creating Consistent and Engaging Content

One of the cornerstones of Kasper's brand-building strategy is the creation of consistent and engaging content. She acknowledges the challenges of producing content regularly, especially as an entrepreneur managing day-to-day operations. "It is a challenge doing that," she admits. However, she emphasises the importance of making time and space for content creation.

Kasper uses a variety of tools to produce and distribute her content, including an iPhone for recording and Premiere Pro for editing. She also utilises platforms like Slack and Infusionsoft for managing her campaigns. "Your goal is to get content under two minutes," she advises, highlighting the importance of being clear, concise, and to the point.

The Role of Audiobooks in Brand Building

In addition to her social media presence and TV appearances, Kasper has also leveraged audiobooks as a key component of her brand. Her audiobooks cover a range of topics, from sales and business to communication skills. "My most popular audiobook is called 'Likeable You,' which is about communication," she says.

These audiobooks are designed to provide quick, actionable insights, typically lasting 30–45 minutes. "I get straight to the point inside my audiobooks," she explains. This format allows her to deliver valuable content without overwhelming her audience, making it easier for them to absorb and apply her advice.

Conclusion

Gail Kasper's journey from uncertainty to becoming a media celebrity offers a wealth of insights for entrepreneurs. Her story underscores the importance of resilience, networking, and consistent content creation in building a successful brand.

"Believe in what it is that you're doing. Believe in the reason that you are doing what you're doing."

For entrepreneurs seeking to get their business noticed, Kasper's experiences provide a roadmap to success.

SCAN TO LISTEN

 GAIL

KASPER

Chapter Twenty-Five
Contra Favours.

DC Palter
Santa Monica, California, USA

"Know your audience and find a way to get in front of them that is probably not the front door."

Taking Techniques from Tech Sales to Sell Books

#DCPalter #NicheMarketing #Entrepreneurship #TechStartups
#Self-publishing #BookMarketing #StartupCulture
#InnovativeMarketing #AudienceEngagement #PersonalBrandBuilding

Introduction

Seasoned tech entrepreneur, author, and Japanophile, DC Palter, lives in Santa Monica, where he has been finding non-traditional ways to market his novel, *To Kill a Unicorn*. Palter is using marketing tactics from his startup days to sell his story about mystery, murder, and bankruptcy, which appeals to a very specific audience; people inside the tech startup community. There are useful lessons to learn as the book industry is notoriously competitive, and self-publishing carries even more challenges.

The Challenge of Marketing a Novel

Palter's experience underscores a universal truth: creating a product, whether a novel or a tech gadget, is only half the battle. "Writing the book's the easy part. Marketing the book is the difficult part," he asserts. This sentiment resonates deeply with entrepreneurs, who often find themselves at a loss once their product is ready for the market.

Lessons from the Tech World

Drawing parallels between his tech ventures and his foray into novel writing, Palter highlights the importance of strategic marketing. "Marketing is two-thirds of the job," he emphasises, a lesson he learned from his days of competing against industry giants like Cisco and Google. For Palter, the key lies in finding and targeting a niche audience.

Finding Your Audience

Palter's novel, a mystery set in the high-tech industry, is not aimed at the general mystery reader. Instead, it targets those familiar with the tech startup world. "The book is not for your typical mystery reader... My audience doesn't read the *New York Times*," he explains. By identifying his specific audience, Palter was able to tailor his marketing efforts effectively.

Leveraging Existing Networks

One of Palter's most successful strategies has been leveraging his existing networks within the tech industry. "I'm in accelerators. I'm in the investment community. I'm writing articles. I'm mentoring these startups," he says. By positioning himself as an authority in the tech world, Palter was able to promote his novel to a receptive audience.

Content Marketing

Palter's approach to content marketing is particularly noteworthy. He began writing articles about what investors look for in pitch decks, publishing them on platforms like Substack and Medium. "I now have 50,000 followers. My articles get read by tens of thousands of people," he notes. Each article ends with a subtle plug for his novel, seamlessly integrating his promotional efforts with valuable content.

The Power of Reviews

Understanding the importance of reviews, Palter devised a clever strategy to garner them. He offers to review pitch decks for startup founders in exchange for purchasing and reviewing his novel.

"You want my time. I want a favour back from you," he states plainly. This reciprocal arrangement not only boosts his book's visibility but also reinforces his authority in the tech community.

Avoiding Common Pitfalls

Palter warns against the allure of paid reviews and marketing services, which often promise much but deliver little. "If you're looking at actually making money from your book, don't waste your time on people offering you their marketing services for the most part," he advises. Instead, he advocates for organic, authentic engagement with one's audience.

Future Endeavours

With the success of *To Kill a Unicorn*, Palter was already gearing up for his next release, *Countdown to Decryption*, a cyber thriller launched in June 2024. This continuity not only keeps his audience engaged but also builds a loyal readership over time.

Conclusion

DC Palter is using some of the low- to no-budget marketing techniques he learnt in his high-tech business to promote his books. The blueprint is the same. Know your audience, leverage existing networks, and offer something in exchange, which has value to both parties but which doesn't cost anyone money.

This could be an oriental piece of wisdom from DC, who spent many years living in Japan.

"Find a way to get in front of your customers... You just may need to find the back door to get there."

SCAN TO LISTEN

 ## DC
PALTER

Chapter Twenty-Six
Gamify Utility.

Karen Frame
Founder and CEO, Makeena, Boulder, Colorado, USA

"We're building a community of brands."

Building a Great Marketplace for Good Products

#KarenFrame #Makeena #SustainabilityInBusiness
#EcoFriendlyShopping #BrandLoyalty #InnovativeMarketing
#ConsumerEngagement #SustainableChoices #GreenBusiness
#DigitalMarketingStrategies

Introduction

From her base in Boulder, Colorado, famous for its outdoors lifestyle, Karen Frame, the founder and CEO of Makeena, is a pioneer in the natural products industry. Makeena, a discovery hub for better-for-you and better-for-the-planet brands, is revolutionising how consumers connect with sustainable products. In a recent conversation, Karen shared her journey, strategies, and insights on building a brand that stands out in a crowded market.

The Genesis of Makeena

Makeena, which means happiness in Swahili, abundance in Hawaiian, and machine in Arabic, is aptly named. "We're a happy abundant machine," Karen explains. The platform serves as a loyalty programme that connects consumers with brands committed to sustainability and health. "We want the consumer to buy better," she says, emphasising the platform's mission to promote products that are good for both people and the planet.

Engaging Consumers with a Community Approach

Karen's vision for Makeena extends beyond a simple loyalty programme. "We're building a community of brands and consumers," she notes. The app, available on iOS and Android, allows consumers to earn rewards such as cash, free products, or swag by engaging with brands. This engagement is crucial for fostering a sense of community and loyalty among users.

One of the standout features of Makeena is its inclusivity. "We show the consumer where you can buy the product... anywhere," Karen explains. Whether it's a local store or an online marketplace like Amazon, Makeena ensures that consumers can access the products they love.

Attracting Brands to the Platform

Getting brands to join Makeena involves a multifaceted approach. Karen leverages her extensive network and industry experience, having started a similar company back in 1994. "We sponsor different groups like Naturally Bolder and Colorado Foodworks," she says. Additionally, Makeena has launched a game show to promote brands, publishes a weekly newsletter on LinkedIn, and participates in trade shows.

"We won a grant from Comcast and there's a little 30-second video running about Makeena on television. It's pretty amazing. There's lots and lots of opportunity out there. You just have to keep open to it."

Karen's personal touch is also a significant factor. "Brands need to know and trust me and then they need to know and trust my team," she asserts. This trust is built through consistent engagement and by showcasing the platform's value proposition.

The Role of the Founder in Brand Building

As a serial entrepreneur, Karen understands the delicate balance between being the face of the brand and allowing it to stand on its own. "As a founder, I'm always looking for really great people to join Makeena on its vision and mission," she says. The goal is to have a team that embodies the brand's values, ensuring its growth and sustainability.

Karen acknowledges that there will come a time when the brand can thrive without her daily involvement. "Once we hit that chasm… I'm going to become hopefully less important," she reflects. However, the founder's vision and mission remain integral to the brand's identity.

Reaching Consumers Through Media and Authenticity

Karen employs a variety of strategies to attract consumers to Makeena. Media appearances, such as discussing rising grocery prices on TV, have proven effective. "Anytime that happens, a ton of people just sign up," she notes. Winning grants, like the one from Comcast, also provides valuable exposure.

Social media is another critical component. Makeena has a presence on platforms like TikTok, Instagram, Twitter, and Facebook. "We have influencers that play that game show, and they win a prize," Karen explains, highlighting the platform's gamified approach to engagement.

Authenticity is at the core of Makeena's marketing strategy. "The reason why I founded the company is because of my personal experience, my personal why," Karen shares. This authenticity resonates with consumers, making the brand more relatable and trustworthy.

Leveraging Technology for Customer Engagement

Makeena's app is designed to make sustainable shopping rewarding and straightforward. Consumers can earn points or cash by scanning barcodes and submitting receipts. "When the balance gets to 20 bucks, they can cash out through PayPal or Venmo," Karen explains. Additional activities, such as taking photos of displays or sharing on social media, also earn rewards.

This gamified approach not only incentivises sustainable shopping but also fosters a deeper connection between consumers and brands. "Our shoppers are super sticky. They love what we're doing," Karen notes.

Conclusion

Karen Frame's journey with Makeena offers valuable lessons for entrepreneurs seeking to get their businesses noticed. By building a community, leveraging personal networks, and maintaining authenticity, Makeena has carved out a unique space in the market.

"If you have a very authentic brand, people will come to it."

SCAN TO LISTEN

 KAREN FRAME

Chapter Twenty-Seven
Blue Ocean.

Christian Espinosa
Medical Device Cybersecurity Expert, Phoenix, Arizona, USA

"If you build up a company and sell the company, then that brand goes away. So, you are kind of starting over if you do not already have your personal brand and personal website."

Building a Personal Brand to Sell the Company

#ChristianEspinosa #Cybersecurity #PersonalBranding
#StrategicAcquisitions #NicheMarketing #BlueOceanStrategy
#EntrepreneurialGrowth #StoryBrand #BusinessLeadership
#TechInnovation

Introduction

It may be a city with year-round sun, desert beauty, and world-class resorts and golf, but Phoenix, Arizona is also the home to a lot of people with enterprise, including Christian Espinoza. Espinoza has a particular focus on cybersecurity and has a wealth of knowledge to share, particularly on the importance of personal branding and effective storytelling in business.

The Importance of Personal Branding

Christian Espinoza, the mind behind Alpine Security, underscores the significance of personal branding for entrepreneurs. "If you build up a company and sell the company, then that brand goes away. So you're kind of starting over if you don't already have your personal brand and personal website," he explains.

Espinoza believes that a personal brand serves as a forward-thinking strategy. It allows entrepreneurs to leverage their journey and contacts, especially when launching new ventures or writing books. "A lot of entrepreneurs have a message or a vision. So if you've already created a personal brand and you want to write a book, then you can leverage the contacts you've got along your journey," he adds.

Balancing Personal and Business Brands

One of the challenges entrepreneurs face is ensuring that their personal brand does not detract from their business. Espinoza offers a nuanced perspective: "I'm a believer that a business is a reflection of the entrepreneur. So, I think if your personal brand is aligned with your business, it shouldn't be a problem." He cautions against sharing overly personal content, suggesting that entrepreneurs maintain a professional image even when building a personal brand.

Espinoza shares a personal experience to illustrate this point. After selling his business to a publicly traded company, he faced scrutiny over his personal brand. "I had to stop doing a lot of the personal promotion because they thought it was detracting away from the parent company," he recalls. This experience highlights the need for entrepreneurs to be mindful of how their personal actions impact their business.

Niche Marketing and the Power of Focus

Espinoza's journey with Alpine Security offers valuable lessons in niche marketing. Initially, he made the mistake of trying to cater to every client, which led to commoditisation and price competition. "I took pretty much every client. I just thought any revenue is good revenue," he admits. This approach, however, proved unsustainable.

The turning point came when Espinoza decided to focus on a specific niche: medical device cybersecurity. "It's more of a blue ocean strategy versus the red ocean strategy I was following before," he explains. By narrowing their focus, Alpine Security was able to land significant contracts and achieve substantial growth. "Once we got one big client, we asked for referrals from them because it's a small industry," he notes.

StoryBrand Framework: Crafting Effective Messaging

A key strategy that Espinoza employed was the StoryBrand framework by Donald Miller. This framework helps businesses understand their customers' problems and position themselves as guides to solve those problems. "It forces you to understand what your character is, who your customer is, what the real problems are that they have," Espinoza elaborates.

Using this framework, Alpine Security was able to refine its messaging and improve its inbound marketing efforts. "We focused on our website and inbound leads. That really helped us take the next leap in growth," he says. The framework's emphasis on making the client the hero of the story, rather than the company, proved to be a game changer.

Enhancing Customer Experience Through Emotional Intelligence

Espinoza's book, *The Smartest Person in the Room*, addresses a common issue in high-tech industries: the gap between high IQ and low EQ (emotional intelligence). In his cybersecurity company, he realised that technical aptitude alone was not enough. "Most of the problems I was having in my organisation, problems with clients and problems internally, were because of a lack of people skills," he observes.

To address this, Espinoza implemented training on communication, emotional intelligence, and other soft skills. "We had clients that we would get as a one-time project, but they wouldn't sign on for an annual contract. I think because they were happy technically with what we delivered, but they weren't wowed by our experience with them," he explains. By improving his team's people skills, Espinoza was able to convert more clients into long-term partners.

Core Values: The Foundation of Organisational Culture

Another critical aspect of Espinoza's strategy was the establishment of core values within his company. Initially sceptical, he came to realise that core values were essential for aligning his team and improving performance. "I used to think core values were just taglines big companies put on the wall," he admits. However, he found that hiring based on core value alignment led to better cultural fit and organisational success.

One of Alpine Security's core values was "own the problem, find the solution." Espinoza would ask potential hires to describe a scenario where they encountered a problem and how they handled it. "If they didn't show any ownership of the problem, then we realised that they're probably not a good fit," he explains.

Conclusion

Christian Espinoza's journey offers invaluable insights for entrepreneurs looking to get their businesses noticed. From the importance of personal branding and niche marketing to the power of storytelling and core values, his strategies provide a roadmap for success.

"Focus on your messaging. Walking through the StoryBrand framework was the most important thing I did. That helped get us that business."

SCAN TO LISTEN

 CHRISTIAN ESPINOSA

Chapter Twenty-Eight
Being Found.

Bart-Jan Leyts
Founder and CEO, Otamiser, Ghent, Belgium

"If you are being found, if you are being seen, you are getting booked."

Algorithms Tell You Where to Sleep

#BartJanLeyts #Optimiser #InnovationInHospitality
#AIHospitality #BookingEngineoptimisation #YoungEntrepreneur
#HotelRevenueManagement #StartupSuccess #DigitalTransformation
#HospitalityIndustry

Introduction

In the tourist destination of Bruges, Belgium, a young entrepreneur is making waves in the hospitality industry. Bart-Jan Leyts, at just 23 years old, founded Otamiser (originally called Loreca), a company that leverages artificial intelligence to enhance revenue for hotels and bed and breakfasts. Despite his youth, Leyts has already managed to sign up nearly 300 hotels across six countries to his innovative platform. His journey offers invaluable lessons for entrepreneurs seeking to get their businesses noticed.

The Genesis of Otamiser

Leyts' entrepreneurial journey began during his university years, driven by a desire to help his parents', struggling bed and breakfast business during the COVID-19 pandemic. "I was majoring in data and finance and started tinkering with ways to improve their revenue," he recalls. This initial experimentation led to the creation of an algorithm designed to optimise a hotel's ranking on online travel agencies (OTAs) like Booking.com and Expedia.

"Otamiser is like SEO for Google, but for OTAs," explains Leyts. "If you're being found, you're getting booked. This changes the whole dynamic of how revenue management for hotels is done."

Overcoming Industry Challenges

Breaking into the traditional hospitality industry was no small feat, especially for a young entrepreneur. Leyts faced scepticism due to his age and the innovative nature of his product. "The average age of a hospitality owner is like twice my age," he notes. "We were the young guys telling them what they need to change."

To overcome this, Leyts focused on proving the efficacy of his algorithm. "We just have to prove ourselves," he says. "It's all about making the things that you're talking about come true."

Building a Brand and Expanding Reach

Leyts' approach to brand building and customer acquisition has been both bold and strategic. He started by sending emails to local hotels, offering his services at a modest rate. "I just wrote an email to them and said, 'Hey, I'm a 20-year-old guy. I can do this. Do you want to work with me?'" This straightforward approach yielded an overwhelming response, validating his business idea.

Word of mouth has played a significant role in Otamiser's growth. "Hoteliers are very familiar with each other," Leyts explains. "But regarding brand building, we had a lot of articles, some podcasts, and a lot of speaking gigs."

Leyts also emphasises the importance of collaboration. "We have a lot of collaborations with local governments and other service providers. If one grows, the other grows with them," he says. This strategy not only builds trust but also amplifies reach.

Navigating Media Relations

Getting media coverage has been another crucial element of Leyts' strategy. He advises entrepreneurs to be proactive in reaching out to the press. "Just write that email to a local press agency, write an email to start an endorsement," he suggests. "If they don't answer, well, whatever. It just costs five minutes of your life."

Leyts' persistence paid off when he secured endorsements from local governments, which significantly boosted his company's credibility. "Whenever you get endorsed by a local government, it builds that trust that you need in the early phases," he notes.

Customised Solutions for Unique Needs

One of the standout features of Otamiser is its customised approach to each client. "We firmly believe that every hotel, every bed and breakfast is unique," says Leyts. "We need to understand their business 100% before we do something."

This tailored approach ensures that Otamiser can effectively optimise each hotel's visibility on OTAs, considering various parameters such as location, sustainability, and operational constraints. "It's all about being seen, being booked," he adds.

The Importance of Community and Networking

For young entrepreneurs, Leyts highlights the importance of finding a supportive community. "The peer group is way different than an entrepreneur who is a bit older," he explains. "Finding people that you can really relate with is very hard."

Leyts actively seeks out different groups and forums where he can connect with other young entrepreneurs. "These are the people that are struggling with the same decisions," he says, emphasising the value of shared experiences and mutual support.

Conclusion

Bart-Jan Leyts' story demonstrates the importance of doing the simple things at the start, proving your concept, building strong relationships, and staying positive.

"You always have a no, but a yes is something you definitely can get."

For entrepreneurs looking to make their mark, the key take away is clear: be proactive, be persistent, and always be ready to prove the value of your offering.

SCAN TO LISTEN

 BART-JAN
LEYTS

Chapter Twenty-Nine
Strategic Commenting.

Jason Tan

Founder, Engage AI, Brisbane, Australia

"Market positioning is really the one that I would say to think about."

AI-Based LinkedIn Engagement App Gets Engagement

#JasonTan #EngageAI #LinkedInStrategy #AICommenting
#SMBGrowth #StrategicEngagement #AIforSMB #NetworkingAI
#ContentEngagement #BusinessNetworkingAI

Introduction

On the east coast of Australia, in Brisbane, Jason Tan says that he is building a "second brain" for his customers. As the founder of Engage AI, Tan has built a user base of over 50,000 customers in less than a year with a marketing budget of under $1,000. He has accomplished the hockey stick growth dreamt of by venture capitalists, without needing to ask any investors for money.

The Genesis of Engage AI

Engage AI was born out of a personal need. Tan, like many business owners, found it increasingly challenging to manage and personalise interactions on LinkedIn as his network grew. "The biggest problem we are solving is for the unnoticed SMB owner to get noticed," Tan explains. Engage AI is a LinkedIn plugin designed to help users engage with their connections through insightful comments, thus fostering meaningful relationships at scale.

The Power of Commenting for Attention

One of the core strategies behind Engage AI is what Tan calls "commenting for attention." This involves making thoughtful comments on posts by prospects or existing clients to garner their attention. "Who doesn't want a bit of engagement when they spend all the time, energy, and money creating a post?" Tan asks rhetorically. By adding value to conversations, users can stand out and build rapport with their target audience.

Focus on LinkedIn

While many social media tools spread their efforts across multiple platforms, Engage AI is laser-focused on LinkedIn. "LinkedIn is one of the very effective channels that SMBs, especially the B2B SMB owner, are using," Tan notes. This focus allows Engage AI to continually innovate and improve its offerings for LinkedIn users, rather than diluting its efforts across other platforms.

Practical Workflow Solutions

Engage AI is designed to save users time and effort. "The first thing Engage AI does is analyse what exactly the post is about," Tan explains. Users can then choose a tone or write a custom prompt to generate a comment that sounds authentic and relevant. This feature is particularly useful for those who outsource their social media management to virtual assistants (VAs). "The biggest problem of having a VA is they don't necessarily have the diversified knowledge on different topics," Tan points out. Engage AI mitigates this issue by ensuring comments are insightful and on-brand.

Overcoming Obstacles

Transitioning from a consulting business to a product-based business was one of the significant challenges Tan faced. "I have to pick up a lot of new skillsets and then equally find the people who build the product for a global audience from day one," he recalls. Another hurdle was getting noticed with a limited budget. Tan's solution was to "eat our own dog food," using Engage AI to comment on posts by the target audience of his target audience. This strategy helped him acquire the first 3,000–5,000 users.

The Secret Sauce

When asked about the secret sauce behind his success, Tan reveals a clever strategy. "The secret sauce is what I call eating our own dog food," he says. Instead of targeting his direct audience, Tan commented on the posts of the target audience of his target audience. "My target audience is the B2B SMB owner. But if I were to acquire a thousand of them, I need to comment on a thousand of them and then the ROI is only $30 if they subscribe. It makes no sense," he explains. By commenting on posts by senior executives at large corporations, Tan ensured that his comments were seen by the SMB owners who were also trying to engage with those executives. This ingenious approach helped him gain visibility and attract users to Engage AI.

The Pitfalls of Advertising

Tan advises caution when it comes to paid advertising. "Advertising is getting really, really expensive these days," he warns. Instead, he recommends focusing on understanding your customer and refining your messaging before investing heavily in PPC campaigns. "If you are not 100% clear about how you are serving your customer, PPC is best to avoid until you figure out your funnel, your key messages, your USP, and exactly how you will be able to retain the client," he advises.

The Importance of Market Positioning

One of the key factors behind Engage AI's success is its clear market positioning. "We are the LinkedIn AI community, or we are the ChatGPT for the LinkedIn community. And it is what we are. And that is all we do," Tan states emphatically. This focus has allowed Engage AI to stand out in a crowded market and gain significant traction.

Conclusion

Jason Tan's journey with Engage AI underscores the importance of strategic focus, customer engagement, and market positioning in building a successful business. His focused approach to leveraging LinkedIn for meaningful interactions offers a blueprint for entrepreneurs looking to get noticed.

"Market positioning is really the one strategy that I would say will move the needle like crazy."

SCAN TO LISTEN

 # JASON TAN

Chapter Thirty
Competitor Collaboration.

Mark Myers
Peak Profit Solutions, Gainesville, Florida, USA

"I showed them how, through our services, they could enhance their own offerings, turning their relationship with clients from transactional to transformational."

Turning Competitors into Affiliates

#MarkMyers #PeakProfitSolutions #TaxConsulting #FinancialServices
#BusinessStrategy #Taxoptimisation #EntrepreneurJourney
#InnovationInFinance #CollaborativeBusiness #TaxAdvisor

Introduction

In Gainesville, Florida, Mark Myers has spent the last 15 years transforming the unglamorous content of tax codes into a profit centre. His journey from managing high-end health clubs and shoe companies to becoming a tax efficiency expert offers valuable lessons for entrepreneurs seeking to get their businesses noticed.

The Journey to Tax Efficiency

Mark Myers' path to becoming a tax efficiency expert was anything but linear. With an academic background in health sciences and business management, Myers initially found success in running other people's businesses. "Regardless of the type of business, whether it be running a high-end health club in New York City or Los Angeles, or running a shoe company, the process was the same," he explains. This process involved driving revenue, managing expenses, and increasing EBITDA margins.

However, Myers realised that his true calling lay in helping business owners navigate the complexities of tax. "I wanted to continue to work as an entrepreneur, but not in this space, but focus on what I've learned, which is how to run a business and how to consult with business owners," he says.

Finding the Niche

Initially, Myers ventured into the financial services space with a focus on insurance. However, he soon realised that even within this niche, he was still competing in a crowded market. The turning point came when he identified a common pain point among business owners: tax inefficiency. "Most every business owner that

I was working with would complain of the tax pain that they had and that they weren't getting resolved via their CPA," Myers recalls.

This realisation led him to explore the 75,000 pages of tax code for opportunities that were often overlooked by CPAs and wealth advisors. "I realised it was an aha moment. This is an area that is unexplored for the most part by wealth advisors and by CPAs," he notes.

Transforming Competitors into Channels

One of Myers' most ingenious strategies has been converting competitors into channels for his business. By offering solutions that complement rather than compete with the services of CPAs and wealth advisors, he turned potential rivals into partners. "I can solve problems for them that would make them look great and also give more value to their clients," he explains.

This approach has been instrumental in building his brand and expanding his reach. "Now I get CPAs that refer other CPAs to me. I get wealth advisors that refer other wealth advisors to me. And of course, clients will refer clients, which is a beautiful thing," Myers says.

Leveraging Automation and Social Media

To amplify his reach, Myers has effectively utilised automation and social media, particularly LinkedIn. He employs a tool called Lead Central to automate his outreach to potential partners. "I started a campaign that just basically every day, it sends out these automated responses because I get to pick in Atlanta, I want to look for people that are in this space. North Carolina, I want to look for people in this space," he explains.

This automated approach has allowed Myers to scale his business without significantly increasing his workload. "With 50% efficiency, at this point, if I turned it up a notch, I would need to continue to work on scaling my business to make sure that I could handle the incoming workflow," he notes.

Building Trust and Engagement

Myers also emphasises the importance of building trust and engagement with potential clients and partners. He uses a customer relationship management tool called Engage Bay to manage his interactions and ensure that he remains responsive to inquiries. "I allow for people to actually book a 15-minute consultation with me. That's completely free. And I let them know that within that 15-minute consultation, I'm likely able to find one or two or three things that they can do to increase their profit via tax reduction," he says.

This approach not only builds trust but also demonstrates the value that Myers can bring to the table. "I've built that pipeline. Now I'm getting lots and lots of connections every week," he adds.

Conclusion

Mark Myers' innovative approach to tax efficiency and his ability to turn competitors into partners offer valuable lessons for entrepreneurs. By identifying unmet needs, leveraging automation, and building trust through engagement, Myers has successfully transformed his business and made tax liability a profit centre.

"I could still stay in this industry. I could still help the business owners that I wanted to help, but I could access them through my competitors."

Thinking differently about who constitutes a potential client is classic lateral thinking out of the playbook of Edward de Bono. It really demonstrates that there are always opportunities, even in seemingly crowded market places.

SCAN TO LISTEN

 ## MARK
MYERS

Chapter Thirty-One
Crowdfunded Community.

Karen Tan
Co-Founder, The Projector, Singapore

"Crowdfunding for us was really important in the context of Singapore because we looked at it not just as a means to raise money, but also to get people behind us to get the word out."

Projecting a Vision to Rejuvenate Old Cinemas

#KarenTan #TheProjectorSG #IndependentCinema #SingaporeCinema #CommunityCinema #FilmCulture #ArtHouse #CinemaLovers #CreativeEntrepreneurship #CulturalHub #MovieTheatreInnovation

Introduction

In the island city state of Singapore, where cinema-going is a national pastime, Karen Tan has carved out a unique niche. As the co-founder and CEO of The Projector, Singapore's only independent cinema, Tan has built a thriving community-based venue that goes beyond just screening films. The former investment banker has used an unusual form of funding to engage audiences in a way that ensured success, even during the tough times.

The Vision Behind The Projector

Karen Tan, along with her co-founders Blaise Trigg-Smith and her sister Sharon Tan, launched The Projector in 2014. The cinema is not just a place to watch films; it's a cultural hub that hosts comedy nights, jazz performances, drag queen cabarets, art exhibitions, and even cat adoption drives.

"The vision was to create a place that was beyond just a space for showing film, but also to broaden our slate of content to anything that was cultural and artistic and creative," says Tan.

Crowdfunding: A Dual-Purpose Strategy

One of the most compelling aspects of The Projector's early days was its approach to funding. The team turned to crowdfunding, raising between $50,000 and $70,000 on Indiegogo. While this amount was not the majority of the funds required, it served a dual purpose.

"Crowdfunding for us was really important in the context of Singapore because we looked at it not just as a means to raise money, but also to get people behind us to get the word out," Tan explains.

This strategy not only provided the necessary seed capital but also created an emotional connection with their early supporters.

"Having people put their money where their mouth is... makes sense that they tell their friends and they get their friends to come once it's open," she adds.

Building a Membership Programme

The Projector has also developed a membership scheme to foster a sense of community and loyalty among its patrons. Members receive free tickets, discounts on merchandise and food, and sometimes exclusive access to special events.

"We do engage a lot with our community on our socials, Facebook, Instagram, there's also now TikTok," says Tan. The cinema also sends out a weekly newsletter with a high open rate of 50%, indicating strong engagement.

Navigating Government Regulations

Operating an independent cinema in a highly regulated environment like Singapore comes with its own set of challenges. The Projector has to comply with stringent regulations, particularly from the Infocomm Media Development Authority (IMDA), Singapore's censorship board.

"Being a cinema operator is a licensed business in Singapore, as with most other places. The simple answer is comply," Tan states. However, she also mentions that they engage with the IMDA to push back on certain censorship decisions, showing that compliance does not mean passivity.

Balancing Corporate and Community Interests

Interestingly, The Projector has managed to attract big corporate clients like Google, Microsoft, and Uber for venue hire, despite its offbeat, arty image. This dual appeal is a testament to the venue's unique charm.

"People like something different, and that's what we are," says Tan. The cinema's vintage 1970s aesthetic and relaxed atmosphere make it an attractive alternative to standard corporate venues.

Learning from Failures

Not everything The Projector has tried has been a success. For instance, they attempted to screen more mainstream films like *Avatar* and *Top Gun* to diversify their offerings. However, this move did not resonate well with their audience.

"We thought, OK, well, if they're showing the exact same film... surely the choice is obvious. The customer will come to us. But no," Tan admits. This experience has led them to reconsider their strategy and focus on what they do best.

Creating Instagrammable Moments

The Projector has also excelled in creating a physical space that encourages social sharing. The walls are adorned with posters of films that have been shown at the cinema, and the lobby features mini sets inspired by certain films.

"We've created a vibe that encourages people to interact with the physical space and also, you know, take photos and share," says Tan. This approach not only enhances the customer experience but also serves as organic marketing.

Engaging the Community in Physical Spaces

One of the most innovative aspects of The Projector is how it involves the community in shaping its physical spaces. During renovations, community members help build signage, paint ceilings, and even sign their names on the walls.

"It's all part of allowing people to contribute to you, as well as have a sense of ownership over what we're creating," Tan explains.

Conclusion

The Projector provides a low-cost and sustainable example of building a community-centric business. From leveraging crowdfunding for both capital and marketing to creating Instagrammable moments and engaging the community in physical spaces, Karen Tan and her co-founders have rejuvenated unused venues. They are also giving people a place and a purpose to come together.

The key take away? "Build a community around your business... These will be your most loyal fan base and ambassadors," says Tan.

SCAN TO LISTEN

 KAREN TAN

Chapter Thirty-Two
Loyal Not Happy.

Charles Read
Founder of GetPayroll, Lewisville, Texas, USA

"There's no traffic jam on the extra mile. Go the extra mile for your clients, go the extra mile for your employees. Your competitors will not do that."

Keep Going and Let Go

#PayrollServices #SmallBusinessSupport #EntrepreneurLife
#TaxCompliance #CustomerService #BusinessGrowth
#DigitalMarketing #BusinessLeadership #ReferralPrograms
#VeteranEntrepreneur

Introduction

In the famous oil city of Dallas, Texas, Charles Read has built a formidable enterprise, GetPayroll, which manages over a billion dollars in payroll annually. From its humble beginnings, Read's company has grown into a national powerhouse, serving businesses across the USA. The silver fox entrepreneur Read explains how he has built the business the traditional way and is growing it with the new way.

The Evolution of GetPayroll

Charles Read's journey with GetPayroll began over 30 years ago, initially as a local business in the Dallas–Fort Worth area. The transition to a national firm came with the advent of the internet in the late 1990s. "We did a lot of door knocking, handing out brochures, talking to people, network meetings," Read recalls. "Most of which is no longer effective. But it worked at the time."

The shift to an online presence was transformative. "When we moved into the internet in the late nineties, we became a national firm almost overnight," he explains. This transition required a significant learning curve, particularly in understanding state tax regulations across the country.

Building Relationships and Brand

One of the cornerstones of GetPayroll's success has been its commitment to personal relationships and brand integrity. "We always made the point that you could call Charles," Read says. "If I'm in the office, I'll take the phone call." This personal touch set GetPayroll apart from its larger, faceless competitors.

Read emphasises the importance of being accessible and maintaining a human connection with clients. "We are a small business that deals with small businesses. We're not a faceless, huge monolith," he asserts. This approach has helped build a loyal customer base, with over 5,000 clients nationwide.

The Role of a Great Team

As GetPayroll grew, Read recognised the need to delegate responsibilities to a capable team. "I've got a great staff," he says. "I hire good, competent people who do excellent work and have great customer skills." This strategy has allowed Read to focus on building the company rather than getting bogged down in day-to-day operations.

Read's philosophy is clear: "An entrepreneur doesn't need to be the smartest person in the room. He needs to hire the smartest person in the room." By surrounding himself with talented individuals, Read has been able to scale his business effectively.

The Power of Marketing

Marketing has played a crucial role in GetPayroll's growth. However, Read admits that it took him some time to realise the importance of professional marketing expertise. "I thought I could market," he says. "Then I hired a marketing manager and realised within a couple of weeks that I couldn't market my way out of a paper bag."

This realisation led to significant changes in GetPayroll's marketing strategy. The new marketing team introduced innovative approaches, particularly in social media. "We actually get hundreds of leads from Facebook, LinkedIn, TikTok, Instagram, YouTube," Read notes. Despite his personal scepticism about social media, Read acknowledges its effectiveness. "It works. And they're in tune with that in a way I'm not."

Embracing Humour and Creativity

One of the more surprising elements of GetPayroll's marketing strategy is the use of humour and creative content. "We do serious ones. We do some that aren't so serious," Read says, referring to their YouTube videos. These include parodies of popular films and fun, engaging content that resonates with a younger audience.

This approach not only makes payroll services more approachable but also helps in building a distinctive brand identity. "We need to be in that world," Read explains. "And I need people who are smart, experienced, and knowledgeable in that world."

Leveraging Referral Programmes

GetPayroll has also implemented a successful referral programme to drive growth. "We have a referral programme for our clients and for anyone, actually," Read says. This programme incentivises referrals by offering a percentage of the revenue on a residual basis. "We're paying out thousands of dollars a month in referral fees, which then generates tens of thousands of dollars a month in revenue."

This strategy has proven to be an effective way to expand their client base while maintaining strong relationships with existing customers.

Exploring New Channels

In addition to traditional marketing methods, GetPayroll has explored new channels to reach potential clients. One innovative approach involved using Fiverr to scrape contact information for insurance agents across the country. "For $50, he scraped every agent for that company in the USA," Read explains. This investment has already yielded significant returns, demonstrating the value of thinking outside the box.

Learning from Failure

Not every strategy has been successful for GetPayroll. Read candidly shares that pay-per-click campaigns have not worked for his business. "We've tried it at least three times. It's been an abject failure every time," he admits. This willingness to experiment and learn from failure is a crucial aspect of entrepreneurial success.

Conclusion

Charles Read's journey with GetPayroll offers a wealth of insights for entrepreneurs. From the importance of personal relationships and a strong team to the power of professional marketing and creative content, his experiences provide a roadmap for building a successful business.

"There's no traffic jam on the extra mile."

By going the extra mile for clients and employees, entrepreneurs can build loyalty and achieve lasting success.

SCAN TO LISTEN

 CHARLES READ

Chapter Thirty-Three
Breathing Success.

Peter Mann
Founder, Oransi, Blacksburg, Virginia, USA

"Most people buy on emotion, and then they justify it rationally with the tech specs and the other things. But that's just human nature."

A Breath of Fresh Air

#PeterMann #B2BMarketing #Oransi #HealthyLiving #IndoorAirQuality #BusinessGrowth #InnovationInBusiness #EcoFriendly #CustomerSatisfaction #AsthmaCare

Introduction

Peter Mann, founder and CEO of Oransi, hails from the picturesque but surprisingly polluted state of Virginia, USA. His journey into entrepreneurship began with a deeply personal mission: to alleviate his son's breathing issues. What started as a quest to improve indoor air quality for his family has since evolved into a multi-million-dollar air purifier business.

From Personal Need to Business Opportunity

Peter Mann's foray into the air purifier market was driven by necessity. "My son struggled with asthma as an infant, and it really left a mark on me," he recalls. This personal experience became the driving force behind Oransi, a company dedicated to improving indoor air quality.

Initially, the market for air purifiers was relatively niche. However, the onset of the COVID-19 pandemic dramatically shifted public awareness and demand. "COVID really changed things, shedding light on the importance of indoor air quality," Peter notes. This surge in demand also brought increased competition, but Peter's background in marketing and operations from his tenure at Fortune 100 tech companies like Tech Data and Dell equipped him to navigate these challenges effectively.

The Importance of Understanding Your Market

One of the key strategies Peter employed was a deep understanding of his market and customers. "It's really difficult when no one knows your brand, you have no reviews. It's like, why should I buy from you?" he explains. Peter emphasises the importance of viewing things from the customer's perspective. "What do they care about? What are their pain points? Can we speak to them in messaging that connects?"

Initially, Oransi started by private labelling products before evolving into designing their own. This gradual approach allowed them to refine their offerings based on customer feedback and market needs. "It's figuring out where you want to go and then working backwards to how you get there," Peter advises.

Transitioning from B2C to Business-to-Business

Interestingly, Oransi's market focus shifted from consumer to business-to-business (B2B) due to changing market dynamics. "When I started, people weren't even thinking about air purifiers in business spaces or schools. It was really COVID that changed it," Peter explains. This shift required a different marketing approach, leveraging his experience in B2B from his time at Tech Data and Dell.

Leveraging Reviews and Building Trust

Despite the B2B focus, Oransi places significant emphasis on customer reviews. "A lot of the folks that are in the B2B segment that are buying air purifiers have never bought them before. They want to have confidence that what they're buying makes sense," Peter says. With over 6,000 reviews on their website, Oransi uses platforms like Yotpo to build trust and credibility. "Most people buy on emotion unless it's a pure commodity. And then they justify it rationally with the tech specs and the other things," he adds.

The Role of Education in Marketing

Education plays a crucial role in Oransi's marketing strategy. "A lot of people that are buying our products have never bought these before. They don't know what they're buying," Peter explains. By providing educational content, Oransi helps customers make informed decisions, thereby building trust and confidence. "It's all around trust and confidence and setting proper expectations for what this is going to do," he notes.

Sustainability as a Marketing Strategy

Sustainability is another cornerstone of Oransi's marketing strategy. "Sustainability is around making the product in an environmentally responsible way. It's about right to repair, which is becoming a really big issue in the USA," Peter explains. By manufacturing locally, Oransi ensures that any broken products can be repaired and sent back, reducing waste. "People want to buy from someone who they share values with," he adds.

Learning from Mistakes

Peter is candid about the challenges and mistakes along the way. One particularly painful experience involved a large overseas order that was cancelled at the last minute. "We never took a deposit on their order just to ensure that they took it. And so we custom built this for them. And we were stuck with this inventory," he recalls. This experience underscored the importance of securing deposits, especially for custom orders.

Embracing AI and Technology

Oransi is also exploring the use of AI and technology to enhance their offerings. "We have some of that data on our website in terms of air quality and pollen, just to provide a resource to our customers," Peter says. Internally, AI is used as a productivity tool, particularly in marketing. "It can come up with some really good ideas for messaging or different ways of seeing something that like, oh, that never occurred to us," he notes.

Conclusion

Peter Mann's journey with Oransi underscores the importance of understanding your market, building trust through reviews and education, and leveraging sustainability as a key differentiator.

"Build marketing into your product because you need to connect with who you're selling to. If you can make something that's differentiated and really solves the customer pain points, it's so much easier to sell that product."

SCAN TO LISTEN

 PETER MANN

Chapter Thirty-Four
Sustainability Stories.

Mathias Boissonot
Founder, Handprint.Tech, Bali, Indonesia

"We've built the brand around challenging the status quo, offering a new perspective on nature."

Creating a Carbon Handprint

#MathiasBoissonot #HandprintTech #SustainableTech
#EcoFriendlyBusiness #GreenInnovation #BaliEntrepreneurs
#EnvironmentalImpact #CorporateSustainability #GreenTechnology
#SustainabilityInAction

Introduction

In the lush, tropical paradise of Bali, Mathias Boissonot, a Frenchman who grew up in Polynesia, is making waves in the world of sustainability and technology. As the co-founder and CEO of Handprint.Tech, Boissonot is on a mission to help over 200 companies achieve their sustainability targets through innovative solutions. His company operates at the intersection of sustainability and technology, providing a platform that enables businesses to make a verified, quantified positive impact on the environment.

The Genesis of Handprint.Tech

Handprint.Tech is not just another tech company; it is a marketplace for positive impact. Boissonot explains, "We develop a technology platform that enables companies to make a positive impact that is verified, quantified, etc., while growing with the planet." The company's name, Handprint, signifies the sum of a company's positive impact, as opposed to its footprint, which denotes negative impact.

Operating from Bali, with headquarters in Singapore and additional operations in Bangkok, Ho Chi Minh, and Lisbon, Handprint.Tech is strategically positioned to address the most critical ecosystems in the Global South. "Being in Indonesia for us is very critical because one of the most vital ecosystems is the mangrove ecosystem that stands from Myanmar to Indonesia," Boissonot notes.

Building the Supply Side

One of the key challenges Handprint.Tech faced was building the supply side of their marketplace. Boissonot and his co-founders leveraged their existing network in the NGO space to kickstart this process. "We started with direct personal connections from them," he says. The company then experienced organic growth as they solved pressing problems for these organisations, such as providing recurring funding without the need for upfront fees.

Handprint.Tech offers NGOs a mobile application to report their activities, which in turn helps them access international funding. "We give their staff a mobile application to report on a daily basis on their activity, basically. In exchange, we give them recurring funding," Boissonot explains. This approach has led to a growing list of projects on their waitlist, which are curated based on relevance, alignment, and urgency.

Educating the Market

Educating the market and building credibility has been another crucial aspect of Handprint.Tech's strategy. Boissonot highlights the importance of going beyond just offering companies a way to make a positive impact. "We wanted to transform this into accessing more strategic budgets from companies," he says. By integrating regeneration into customer experiences, Handprint.Tech has demonstrated tangible business value.

For instance, in the e-commerce sector, Handprint.Tech's integration increased cart conversion by 16% through A/B testing. "It increases sales directly," Boissonot states. Similarly, in the advertising industry, their partnership with Teads showed a 9% increase in ad recall. "We are integrating into the iBanking environments of four banks to see how we can make it really ROI positive for those banks," he adds.

Leveraging Social Media and Content

Handprint.Tech has effectively used LinkedIn as a primary channel for communication and brand building. "We communicated a lot on LinkedIn specifically. That has been an amazing channel for us,"

Boissonot reveals. By challenging the status quo of sustainability and offering a new perspective, they have created a strong voice in the industry.

The company also provides educational content through their YouTube channel, white papers, and blog posts. "We are offering this new perspective of looking at the atmosphere, the biosphere, the anthroposphere, the lithosphere, and the hydrosphere," Boissonot explains. This holistic approach to sustainability has resonated well with their audience.

Overcoming Challenges

Like any entrepreneurial journey, Handprint.Tech has faced its share of challenges. Initially, the company focused on solving a problem for the e-commerce sector, which did not align well with their core strengths. "We were focusing on trying to solve a problem that we're not super aligned with," Boissonot admits. The market eventually guided them towards larger companies that required their level of sophistication.

This shift required Handprint.Tech to adapt their product and approach, moving from a low-touch SaaS platform to a high-touch B2B model. "It took us a lot of time to actually execute that shift and deliver on this new company that we've become," Boissonot reflects.

Effective Acquisition Strategies

One of Handprint.Tech's most effective acquisition strategies has been generating introductions. "We ask for two introductions systematically," Boissonot says. By leveraging their network and asking for referrals, they have been able to generate a significant number of leads. "There is nothing better than warm introductions from investors or clients," he emphasises.

Conclusion

Handprint.Tech has built a strong brand in the sustainability space by leveraging personal networks, educating the market, and effectively using social media.

For entrepreneurs, the key take away is clear: focus on providing value, leverage your network for introductions, and use educational content to build credibility and engage your audience.

"The more value we provide to our audience and our ecosystem, the more we can amplify this new way of calculating and thinking about sustainability."

SCAN TO LISTEN

 MATTHIAS
BOISSONOT

Chapter Thirty-Five
Regulated Opportunities.

Jamie Marshall
Founder, Everon IT Services, Leeds, Yorkshire, UK

"Regulated industries are more tightly governed and forced into change more often."

Clients Who Have to Spend

#JamieMarshall #Everon #ITManagedServices #UKTech #B2BTechnology #TechInnovation #ContentMarketing #CustomerServiceExcellence #ITSupport #SustainableIT

Introduction

Jamie Marshall is building Everon to be recognised as one of the top 50 IT managed services companies in the UK. Based in Leeds, Marshall has discovered a profitable niche, regulated industries. Jamie's story also includes the clever use of brownies, instead of cookies, to grow his business.

The Importance of Niching

Jamie Marshall's decision to focus on regulated industries such as financial services, not-for-profits, and legal sectors has been a cornerstone of Everon's success. Initially, Everon attempted to be "everything to everyone," but this approach proved unsustainable. "We were kind of a jack of all trades and a master of none," Jamie admits. The turning point came when they realised that regulated industries, which are more tightly governed and forced into change more often, aligned perfectly with their ethos of forward thinking and continual improvement.

"One of the reasons in particular we chose regulated industries is because they're more tightly governed, they're forced into change more often than a kind of unregulated business or industry," Jamie explains. This strategic focus not only allowed Everon to specialise but also to add more value to their clients, who are often more aware of the pains that come from data breaches or not keeping set standards.

Educating Rather Than Selling

One of the standout aspects of Everon's marketing strategy is their focus on education rather than self-promotion. Jamie believes in being transparent and open, providing clients with the tools and knowledge they need to make informed decisions. This is evident in the resources available on Everon's website, such as the IT energy cost calculator and the business downtime cost calculator.

"The calculators came about from the need to show people what something would look like or would cost them without them kind of having that insight straight away," Jamie says. These tools help clients understand the financial implications of their IT setups, fostering trust and positioning Everon as a knowledgeable partner rather than just a service provider.

Leveraging Content and Technology

Creating valuable content is another pillar of Everon's marketing strategy. Despite being a small team, Everon manages to produce a wealth of articles and resources. Jamie reveals that they work with marketing content feeds within their industry and sometimes use AI to adapt content to fit their culture and values. "We have basically a brand values and a culture piece that we share with anybody or we run past the content we create or the content we adapt," he notes.

This approach ensures that all content aligns with Everon's ethos of being transparent, educational, and open. Jamie is also cautious about avoiding fear-based marketing, preferring to engage clients through genuine interest and helpful information.

Transparency in Pricing and Service

Transparency extends to Everon's pricing and customer service as well. Their website features detailed pricing plans and multiple contact options, including phone numbers and online chat. This openness is part of their commitment to being accessible and trustworthy. "We have a big emphasis on documentation internally," Jamie explains, highlighting their use of IT Glue to manage documentation and standard operating procedures.

This meticulous approach to documentation ensures that Everon can handle a wide range of client requests efficiently. "If a particular scenario occurs, somebody calls up and they want something we don't have a process for, we don't have an understanding of, the first time we do it, we'll document and learn it," Jamie says. This continual improvement process helps Everon maintain high standards of service.

Personal Touch in Customer Engagement

Jamie also emphasises the importance of personal touch in customer engagement. One of their unique strategies is the "impact box," a branded box filled with educational material and personalised items. Jamie recounts a memorable instance where he sent a box of brownies to a potential client after learning about a humorous LinkedIn post involving the client's mother sending brownies to a job interview.

"I googled all the different brownie shops or places to buy brownies in Leeds, found the ones with the best reviews and filled this box full of brownies with a tiny bit of Everon material," Jamie shares. This thoughtful gesture not only caught the client's attention but also laid the foundation for a lasting relationship.

Learning from Mistakes

Like any entrepreneur, Jamie has faced challenges and setbacks. One of the key lessons he learned was the importance of consistency in marketing efforts. In the early days, Everon experimented with various marketing strategies but didn't stick with any long enough to see significant results. "We were probably really naive in thinking that spending 3,000 miles a month on Google ads was going to generate X in a matter of weeks," Jamie reflects.

Understanding the long buying cycle of their clients was crucial in refining their marketing approach. Now, Everon uses tools like PipeDrive for sales and Force24 for marketing automation to track and nurture leads effectively.

Building a Personal Brand

Jamie is also focused on building his personal brand as the face of Everon. He aims to be as personable and approachable as possible, engaging with prospects through various mediums, including speaking at events and participating in podcasts. "I want to grow Jamie Marshall as the face of Everon," he says. By establishing trust and authority, Jamie hopes to create long-term relationships that will benefit Everon.

Conclusion

Jamie Marshall's journey with Everon offers valuable insights for entrepreneurs looking to get their businesses noticed. From the importance of niching and educating clients to leveraging content and maintaining transparency, Jamie's strategies are both practical and effective. His emphasis on transparency, honesty, and continual improvement further sets Everon apart in the competitive IT services industry.

"There's a lot of 'fear, uncertainty and doom', content, which we avoid doing. We want people to engage with us because they're really interested in what we're doing."

SCAN TO LISTEN

 JAMIE
MARSHALL

Chapter Thirty-Six
Packaging Counts.

Jade Gray
Founder, Off-Piste Provisions, Auckland, New Zealand

"The best time to raise money is when you don't need it."

The Entrepreneur and the Pea

#JadeGray #OffPisteProvisions #PlantBased #SustainableEating
#NewZealandBusiness #FoodTech #EcoFriendly #MeatAlternatives
#SustainableFood #ClimateAction

Introduction

Jade Gray, a Kiwi entrepreneur now living on the idyllic Waiheke Island, New Zealand, has embarked on a remarkable journey from running a cattle feedlot in China to pioneering the plant-based meat alternative industry. As the founder of Off-Piste Provisions, Gray is not only transforming the food sector but also offering invaluable lessons on funding, brand building, and customer engagement.

From Cattle Feedlots to Plant-Based Provisions

Gray's journey began in 1996 when he moved to China to manage a cattle feedlot operation. His career in the meat industry saw him working with giants like McDonald's and Costco. However, a growing disillusionment with the sector led him to pivot towards sustainability. "I lost passion, interest in the sector. I got to see under the hood and I wasn't that inspired," Gray recalls.

This epiphany led him to explore plant-based alternatives, driven by the realisation that animal products have a significantly larger carbon footprint compared to plant-based options. "Animal products just had such a larger footprint than plant-based in real terms. We're talking, you know, eight to ten times larger footprint for the same equivalent of nutrition," he explains.

The Genesis of Off-Piste Provisions

Upon returning to New Zealand in 2019, Gray identified a pressing need to address the country's greenhouse gas emissions, half of which come from livestock. Off-Piste Provisions was born out of this necessity, utilising pea protein and advanced food technology to create meat alternatives like beef jerky without the beef. "We effectively used pea protein and some really smart food technology to mimic meat," says Gray.

The name Off-Piste Provisions reflects Gray's love for the outdoors and the company's innovative approach. "I've always loved the outdoors, and I was looking at the next chapter and how do I bring outdoors back into my life," he shares. The brand's products boast an 18-month shelf life, making them ideal for outdoor enthusiasts.

Navigating Challenges and Building a Business

Building a business is fraught with challenges, and Gray's experience is no exception. Returning to New Zealand after two decades in China presented a reverse culture shock. "It was definitely the first kind of awakening. It was like, okay, this is a new game again, so time to learn," he admits.

Without a food background, Gray solved the problem by partnering with food scientists in Singapore.

"I think that marriage of having a consumer-centric design process, which is where I come in, and then having a food technology science approach very much, which is where the science team come in, it really creates that friction you need to come up with great innovation."

The COVID-19 pandemic further complicated matters, disrupting production and market launch plans. Drawing on his experience from the SARS outbreak in China, Gray emphasises the importance of making decisions based on imperfect information during crises. "If you wait, you pretty much die. I took the front foot during COVID and we just ploughed ahead," he asserts.

Marketing Strategies: Packaging and Targeting

Gray's marketing acumen is evident in Off-Piste Provisions' packaging strategy. Despite being a plant-based product, the packaging features images of cows, a deliberate choice to attract meat reducers rather than vegans. "Our target market actually are meat reducers. They're not vegans. They're people who eat meat who are trying to eat less meat," Gray explains.

The packaging is designed to stand out on the shelf and catch the attention of consumers looking for meat jerky. "You need to have the packaging doing the heavy lifting. So catching people's attention is key," he advises.

Distribution and Community Building

Off-Piste Provisions has achieved impressive distribution, with over 700 locations in New Zealand, expansion into Australia, and a presence on Amazon in the USA. Gray attributes this success to a clear marketing strategy and understanding the target consumer. "You need to have a really clear marketing strategy and where a consumer sits, where do they shop, where do they hang out," he notes.

Social media plays a role, but Gray emphasises the importance of community building over sheer numbers. "We're not about just numbers, we're about engagement. And that takes a long time," he says. Mainstream media has also been a crucial tool, particularly for reaching Generation X and baby boomers, the key meat reducers.

Talent and Team Building

Gray's approach to talent acquisition is rooted in building trust and relationships. "I definitely call myself the chief recruitment officer for the first two years of any startup," he states. He stresses the importance of aligning employees' aspirations with the company's goals and identifying skills gaps early on.

Raising Funds and Maintaining Relationships

Raising funds for a niche category from a remote location like Waiheke Island might seem daunting, but Gray's strategy is straightforward: keep in touch with mentors and potential investors. "I've always kept in touch with mentors and people who I've come across on the journey and who I was inspired by," he says.

Gray's consistent communication with his network paid off, allowing him to raise $1.5 million in less than 24 hours. "It wasn't because of a great idea or because I'm an incredibly gifted entrepreneur. It was just because I kept in touch with people who believed in me," he humbly admits.

Conclusion

Jade's business demonstrates the importance of partnerships, packaging, understanding customer motivation, and targeted distribution. He is successfully leveraging mainstream media to build the brand, while at the same time maintaining strong relationships with investors to ensure that funds are always available.

But it's not all been plain sailing.

"We tend to fail fast and just move on. Sometimes the things just don't align, and you just got to move on. And so, I tell my team, let's celebrate the failures, move on."

SCAN TO LISTEN

 JADE
GRAY

Chapter Thirty-Seven
Main Street Marketing.

Terresa Zimmerman
Founder, Business & Brand Strategist, Consultant, Entrepreneur,
Advisor & Award-Winning Author, WOOD Underwear LLC, Raleigh–
Durham–Chapel Hill Area, North Carolina, USA

"I drove around Los Angeles and I walked into stores and asked the buyers if they wanted to see my underwear."

A Woman in Men's Underwear

#TerresaZimmerman #WoodUnderwear #SustainableFashion #MensBasics #EcoFriendly #FashionInnovation #EntrepreneurJourney #RetailStrategy #MainStreetBusiness #SustainableTextiles

Introduction

Terresa Zimmerman, founder of Wood Underwear, is a female entrepreneur living quite literally in a man's world. She is building an underwear brand addressing the poorly supported men of this world and trying to build a brand on main street instead of Amazon. Without experience in the industry, and adopting innovative fabrics, she's created a big marketing challenge for herself and her startup brand.

The Genesis of Wood Underwear

Zimmerman's transition from a tech PR doyenne in Asia to the founder of a men's underwear brand is nothing short of fascinating. "I was just at a point in my career where I thought, I want to work on my stuff. I want to own something," she explains. This desire for ownership and personal investment led her to create Wood Underwear, a brand that now boasts over 500 stores.

The unique selling proposition of Wood Underwear lies in its fabric – Tencel Modal, a wood viscose made from beech tree cellulose. "It's an amazing fibre, with superior wicking, thermo control, odour control, all of the yumminess," Zimmerman enthuses. This blend of cotton and Tencel Modal offers technical properties that make the underwear both comfortable and sustainable.

The Challenge of Entering a New Market

Transitioning from PR to men's underwear was not without its challenges. Zimmerman recalls, "I've been trying to get into men's underwear my whole life." Her humour aside, the real challenge was convincing men to rethink their underwear choices. "Men are not taught to diversify their underwear drawer," she notes. By educating men on the importance of wardrobing – choosing underwear based on the occasion and outfit – Zimmerman has carved out a niche in a crowded market.

Building Relationships Over Transactions

One of the most striking aspects of Zimmerman's strategy is her decision to avoid selling on Amazon. "I fell in love with Main Street," she says. Her focus on building relationships with small business owners and buyers has been a cornerstone of her success. "It's relationship-driven," she emphasises. This approach has allowed her to create a brand that resonates deeply with its customer base.

Zimmerman's commitment to Main Street is evident in her personal approach to sales. "I walked into stores and asked the buyers if they wanted to see my underwear," she recalls. This hands-on method not only secured her first orders but also laid the foundation for long-term relationships.

The Importance of Authenticity

Zimmerman's journey has not been without its missteps. One significant lesson she shares is the danger of outsourcing sales too early. "I tried to outsource my sales and it was a very expensive mistake," she admits. The lack of personal investment from external sales teams meant that her product was not given the attention it deserved. "You can't give it away," she warns. This experience underscored the importance of being directly involved in the sales process, especially in the early stages.

Leveraging Media and Trade Shows

Media relations have played a crucial role in getting Wood Underwear noticed. Zimmerman's background in PR has undoubtedly been an asset. "We produce educational materials for them to talk about wardrobing and what the proper underwear does," she explains. By providing valuable content, she has been able to engage both store owners and customers effectively.

Trade shows have also been a vital part of her strategy. "We go to trade shows. I went to a lot of trade shows I had no business at," she admits. While some were costly and unproductive, others provided invaluable opportunities to build relationships and showcase her brand.

Giving Back: A Core Value

From the outset, giving back has been integral to Wood Underwear's ethos. Partnering with One Tree Planted, the company plants a tree for every order placed on their website. "1% of every wholesale order goes to planting trees," Zimmerman states. This commitment to sustainability not only aligns with the brand's values but also resonates with a growing segment of eco-conscious consumers.

Conclusion

Zimmerman's tenacity and creativity in building the Wood Underwear brand demonstrate that ingenuity is a substitute for money.

As Zimmerman herself puts it, "You have to find ways to do things that you can afford that are a little bit different."

SCAN TO LISTEN

 TERRESA
ZIMMERMAN

Chapter Thirty-Eight
Ethical Business.

Jill Poet
Co-Founder and CEO, Organisation for Responsible Business,
Southend-on-Sea, Essex

"Doing good is good for business."

Do No Evil

#JillPoet #EthicalBusiness #ResponsibleBusiness #Sustainability
#CorporateResponsibility #UKBusiness #EnvironmentalImpact
#SocialGood #BusinessEthics #ConsumerDemand

Introduction

"Do No Evil" isn't enough anymore. Companies must proactively "do good," and be seen to be playing their role at all levels of society. Jill Poet, co-founder and CEO of the Organisation for Responsible Business (ORB) in the UK, offers a refreshing perspective on how businesses can get noticed by being responsible and authentic. Her insights are not just theoretical; they are grounded in over a decade of experience helping businesses integrate ethical practices into their core operations.

The Importance of Responsibility in Business

"Doing good is good for business," Jill asserts, a mantra that has only grown more relevant over the years. In today's market, consumers and clients are increasingly inclined to support businesses that demonstrate a genuine commitment to social and environmental responsibility. "Whoever your client is, they are increasingly wanting to buy products and services from businesses that care about people and the environment," she explains.

Jill emphasises that it's not enough to merely engage in responsible practices; businesses must also communicate these efforts effectively. "I've come across loads of businesses that do really good stuff, but if I look at their website or their LinkedIn profile, it doesn't tell me," she notes. Transparency and communication are key to leveraging responsible practices as a marketing tool.

Avoiding the Pitfalls of Greenwashing

One of the significant risks in promoting responsible business practices is the accusation of greenwashing – making misleading claims about the environmental benefits of a product or service.

Jill is acutely aware of this danger and advocates for authenticity. "It's got to be authentic," she stresses. "If you say anything, think about, if anyone questions this, can I have evidence to prove what I've said is true?"

The new Green Claims Act in the UK aims to enforce this authenticity, ensuring that businesses can substantiate their claims. Jill advises businesses to be cautious and to ensure that their responsible practices are genuinely integrated into their operations, rather than being superficial marketing ploys.

Tools for Small Businesses

Jill's organisation offers practical tools to help businesses of all sizes, particularly small enterprises, to navigate the complexities of responsible business practices. ORB provides an online course designed to help businesses assess their current practices and identify areas for improvement. "It's designed to help you to think about what's appropriate for your business," she explains. The course covers various aspects, including employee support, community engagement, supply chain impact, and environmental footprint.

Jill acknowledges that small businesses have limited capacity and resources. Therefore, the course is tailored to help them focus on what is feasible and impactful for their specific context. "There isn't a one-size-fits-all benchmark," she says. The goal is to help businesses identify their strengths and areas for improvement, and to communicate these effectively to their stakeholders.

The Role of Authenticity and Accountability

In an era where social media and NGOs hold businesses accountable, authenticity has become more critical than ever. "People aren't interested in you doing bright, shiny things unless those shiny things also equate to those core values in your business," Jill observes. This shift towards genuine, value-driven business practices is not just a trend but a necessity for long-term success.

Jill also highlights the growing importance of Environmental, Social, and Governance (ESG) in the corporate world. While this term may be more familiar in larger businesses, the principles apply universally. "To be a responsible business, you absolutely need to be proactively trying to make a positive difference in terms of people and environment," she asserts.

Cost and Profitability of Responsible Practices

Contrary to the belief that responsible business practices are costly, Jill argues that they can be highly cost-effective, especially for small businesses. "You do not need any budget at all when you are doing corporate social responsibility as a small business properly," she states. The focus should be on core values rather than expensive projects.

Jill provides practical advice on starting with no-cost or low-cost initiatives, particularly in environmental sustainability. "You can start by doing no-cost, low-cost things, and then re-fence the money that you are saving," she suggests. This approach allows businesses to gradually invest in more significant sustainability measures without straining their finances.

Impact on Employee Engagement

Responsible business practices also play a crucial role in attracting and retaining talent. Millennials, now the largest demographic in the workforce, are particularly discerning about the values of their employers. "They are far more concerned about who they are working for and what their values are," Jill notes.

Several ORB members have left lucrative careers to start their own businesses, driven by a desire to align their work with their values. "We will only work with ethical business or values-based businesses," is a common refrain among these new entrepreneurs. This alignment not only attracts like-minded clients but also creates a more fulfilling work environment.

Getting Noticed as a Responsible Business

Jill practices what she preaches, using various strategies to get ORB noticed. "We have to talk about what we're doing, the purpose behind it, our values," she says. Social media, particularly LinkedIn, plays a significant role in their outreach efforts. Additionally, Jill emphasises the importance of a compelling "About Us" page on the company website, which should highlight what makes the business unique.

Awards and certifications can also enhance a business's credibility, but Jill cautions against "badge collecting." "Make sure that it has real value, because if it hasn't, if you've just collected something where you ticked a box, people can see through that," she advises.

Real-World Examples

Jill shares inspiring examples of businesses that have successfully integrated responsible practices. One notable case involves a marketer who shifted her focus from corporate clients to more values-aligned businesses. "All of a sudden, these corporate businesses were coming to her and asking her to do work for them," Jill recounts. This marketer's commitment to authenticity attracted clients who genuinely wanted to improve their sustainability practices.

Conclusion

Jill Poet's insights offer a compelling case for integrating responsible practices into business operations. For entrepreneurs seeking to get noticed, the key take away is clear: authenticity, responsibility, and effective communication are not just ethical imperatives but powerful marketing strategies. By embedding these principles into their core values, businesses can attract clients, engage employees, and achieve long-term success.

As Jill says, "Clients – irrespective of their sector – increasingly prefer to engage with businesses that demonstrate genuine concern for societal and environmental issues."

SCAN TO LISTEN

 # JILL POET

Chapter Thirty-Nine
Speedy Delivery.

Izzy Rosenzweig
Founder and CEO, Portless, Ontario, Canada

"It was about showing, not telling. Each successful delivery, each satisfied end customer, built our case."

Improve Customer Experience by Going Portless

#IzzyRosenzweig, #Portless, #SupplyChainInnovation, #EcommerceSolutions, #ShippingSimplified, #GlobalLogistics, #DirectToConsumer, #TechInLogistics, #SustainableShipping, #Entrepreneurship.

Introduction

Izzy Rosenzweig comes from a family of entrepreneurs who were shipping goods around the world. It was inevitable that he would find a better solution to the time and costs being spent on logistics. As the founder of Portless, Rosenzweig has developed a business model that promises to alleviate the perennial headaches associated with shipping and logistics, particularly for direct-to-consumer (DTC) brands. His service promises the best brand experience for customers and cost savings for the entrepreneur.

The Genesis of Portless

Rosenzweig's journey into the world of supply chain management began out of necessity. "I started doing this as a brand myself," he explains. "We shipped millions and millions of products in this model." The traditional method of shipping goods – producing large quantities, loading them into containers, and enduring lengthy shipping times – was fraught with inefficiencies. "Instead of a brand making 5,000 t-shirts, putting them on a container, and waiting anywhere from 30 to 60, sometimes 90 days to get to a port, you could skip all of that," he says.

Portless offers a streamlined alternative. By acting as a third-party logistics provider (3PL) based in China, Portless can pick, pack, and ship products directly to consumers in under six days. This model eliminates the need for brands to tie up capital in inventory and endure long shipping times. "We could ship it to your customer within six days in the United States with a fully local experience," Rosenzweig notes. "Customer gets a USPS tracking number within one day of the order, and it gets delivered by a USPS driver."

The Evolution of a Business Model

The concept behind Portless is not entirely new, but its execution has reached new heights in recent years. "This model's been around for about 10 years, but it's only gotten really good the last two and a half years," Rosenzweig explains. Early iterations of the model were plagued by long delivery times and poor customer experiences. However, recent advancements have made it a viable option for modern e-commerce businesses. "The last two and a half years, it's gotten really good, where not only is delivery time to the United States under six days, but also the experience is 100% local."

Enhancing the Customer Experience

One of the critical aspects of Portless's service is its focus on the customer experience. "We take that part super seriously because we were a brand for 10 years," Rosenzweig emphasises. The company works closely with brands to ensure that the packaging and presentation of their products meet high standards. "We had a customer that we onboarded, and we said, 'By the way, your packaging has a logo on it, why don't we go a little further?'" The result was a beautifully designed, eco-friendly envelope that cost significantly less to produce in China than it would have in the United States. "Their customers started to post the packaging more than the product," Rosenzweig recalls.

The Mechanics of Portless

For those unfamiliar with the intricacies of supply chain management, the term 3PL might seem opaque. A 3PL is a company that offers outsourced logistics services, which encompass anything that involves the management of one or more facets of procurement and fulfilment activities. In the case of Portless, this means handling everything from picking and packing to shipping and delivery.

The process is straightforward yet revolutionary. Companies can have their goods sent from the factory in China directly to the Portless logistics centre. From there, the goods are shipped directly to the consumer. This approach saves both time and money, allowing vendors to either take the extra profit or pass on the savings to the consumer. "Instead of you waiting all that time, money tied up in inventory on the boat, we could ship it to your customer within six days," Rosenzweig explains.

Marketing and Brand Building

Transitioning from a consumer-focused business to a B2B model required a shift in marketing strategy for Rosenzweig. "When I ran the consumer side of the business, I never put my face to the brand," he says. However, marketing to business owners necessitated a more personal approach. "I'm doing podcasts, I join communities, I contribute. How can I help with marketing ideas? How can we help with packaging ideas, with cash flow ideas?"

Rosenzweig also leverages social media platforms like LinkedIn and Twitter to share insights and engage with the community. "I'm always posting multiple times a week, interesting stuff about supply chain, the history of supply chain, how people could look at supply chain differently," he notes. This strategy has proven effective in building the Portless brand and establishing Rosenzweig as a thought leader in the industry.

Lessons Learned

Rosenzweig's journey has not been without its challenges. One significant learning experience came from his initial foray into digital marketing. "We were always told Google, Google, Google, this is where you've got to live," he recalls. However, he soon realised that this approach was not yielding the desired results. "Our products were discovery products. They're unique products, interesting products. So no one searches unique because they've never seen it before."

Instead, Rosenzweig found greater success on discovery platforms like Facebook, Instagram, TikTok, and Pinterest. "For us, we poured a lot of money into Google. It didn't have good ROI," he admits. The key take away? "Every business is unique. Every business is different. Sure, take in advice, but then filter it and say, okay, does this make sense for you?"

The Future of E-Commerce

Rosenzweig is optimistic about the future of e-commerce and the role that Portless will play in it. "This is 1980s all over again," he says, drawing a parallel to the transformative impact of containerisation on global trade. "If you're in e-commerce, you're in digital retail, it makes no sense. Why bring it to your warehouse, unpack it, and repack to then ship again? We could deliver it to your customer in the exact same timeline that you're doing it today, but you have all the benefits."

For entrepreneurs looking to optimise their supply chain and improve their cash flow, Portless offers a compelling solution.

"You have way better cash flow, you're saving money, potentially in import duties. You can serve international markets with just a click of a button in Shopify markets," Rosenzweig explains.

Conclusion

Izzy Rosenzweig's Portless is eliminating the inefficiencies of traditional supply chain models and allows brand owners to focus on what they do best, creating and marketing their products.

"The magic is in the supply chain. How it improves your cash flow. How it improves your lead times. By changing the way that products are shipped to customers, entrepreneurs can save money and time, and improve the customer experience of the brand."

SCAN TO LISTEN

 IZZY
ROSENWEIG

Chapter Forty
Discrete Networking.

Mathieu Johnsson
Founder, Marble Drones, Melksham, Wiltshire, UK

"When you get in front of high-level decision makers, inevitably, they're going to look for your online presence."

Drones to Rescue the Oceans

#MathieuJohnsson, #MarbleDrones, #DroneTechnology, #MarineConservation, #OceanMonitoring, #SustainableOceans, #AerospaceInnovation, #EnvironmentalTech, #MaritimeDrones, #TechForGood.

Introduction

A French engineer named Mathieu Johnsson is quietly revolutionising the way we monitor marine environments. Formerly an aerospace engineer at Airbus, Johnsson holds an MSc in Aerospace Vehicle Design from Cranfield University and is based in Wiltshire, England. His company, Marble, is pioneering the use of drones to monitor vast marine areas, addressing critical environmental and security challenges.

From Childhood Passion to Aerospace Innovation

Mathieu Johnsson's journey began with a childhood fascination for planes. "I have pictures of me when I was two years old sitting on top of a stack of pillows next to my dad flying a general aviation plane," he recalls. This early passion led him to a career in aerospace engineering, but he soon found himself disillusioned with the stagnation in the field. "Large planes haven't changed much in the past 50 years," he notes. This realisation spurred him to explore the burgeoning field of unmanned aviation, ultimately leading to the creation of Marble.

The Birth of Marble

Marble was born out of a necessity to innovate in a niche market. "In the UK, there weren't that many companies you could work for in that space," Johnsson explains. His company focuses on using drones to monitor marine environments, a task he describes as "the hardest problem because it's a very, very large area and you need to monitor it constantly." The United Nations aims to protect 30% of the planet's marine areas by 2030, but current monitoring methods are inadequate. Marble aims to fill this gap by providing scalable, cost-effective solutions.

Overcoming Marketing Challenges

One of the most intriguing aspects of Johnsson's strategy is his approach to marketing. Unlike consumer-focused businesses, Marble's primary clients are governments and nonprofits. "How do you build the brand of Marble? Because plainly you're selling to governments rather than consumers," he ponders. The answer lies in persistence and strategic targeting. "We kept going. That's how we made it happen," he says, emphasising the importance of resilience.

Initially, Marble sought R&D funding through defence frameworks but quickly realised the limitations. "You don't want to become dependent on that R&D money because that usually doesn't lead to actually any procurement," Johnsson advises. Instead, Marble pivoted to selling to smaller governments and nonprofits, which proved to be a more viable strategy. "We ended up selling to nonprofits, which was an ideal starting point because we could provide, even with a prototype, something of very high value to them," he explains.

The Importance of a Compelling Story

A compelling narrative is crucial for any business, and Marble is no exception. The name "Marble" itself is a testament to this. "The name Marble came from the official name of the first picture taken of the Earth from space, called the Blue Marble," Johnsson reveals. This iconic image has long been associated with sustainability, aligning perfectly with Marble's mission. "I wanted a name that resonates with environmental protection and decarbonisation," he adds.

Navigating Regulatory Hurdles

Operating drones, especially over marine environments, comes with its own set of regulatory challenges. "Drones need to be constantly monitored by a pilot on the ground, and that pilot needs to be able to see the drone," Johnsson explains. This limitation makes it difficult to monitor vast marine areas. Marble's solution? Focus on markets with fewer regulatory constraints. "One of the reasons we went for marine monitoring is that there are a lot less people flying above water," he says. This strategic choice has allowed Marble to operate more freely and effectively.

Scaling the Business

As Marble continues to grow, Johnsson is keen on scaling the business by focusing on data rather than hardware. "What we're selling is not actually the drone. We're selling the data," he clarifies. This approach mirrors the satellite imagery market, where customers purchase data rather than owning the satellites. "We will be operating drones on behalf of everyone else, collecting the data, and then we'll sell it through a web interface," he elaborates. This model not only reduces costs but also makes the technology accessible to a broader range of clients.

Lessons Learned and Future Directions

Reflecting on his journey, Johnsson acknowledges the importance of building a strong online presence. "When you get in front of high-level decision-makers, inevitably, they're going to look for your online presence. And if you have very little, that can be detrimental," he admits. This insight has prompted him to invest more in marketing and brand building, even though Marble's primary audience is not the general public.

Conclusion

Johnsson's passion for aerospace and environmental sustainability has been the driving force behind Marble's success, proving that a clear vision and relentless pursuit can overcome even the most daunting challenges.

"Pick something that you're really going to care about, and you really want whatever you're building to happen in the world, and that's going to keep you going when it's tough."

SCAN TO LISTEN

 MATHIEU

JOHNSSON

Chapter Forty-One
Game Mindset

Dre Baldwin
Founder, Work on Your Game, Inc., Miami, Florida, USA

"If you don't have a clear destination, then there is nothing to focus on."

Work on Your Game to Build Your Business

#DreBaldwin #WorkOnYourGame #EntrepreneurMindset
#BusinessCoaching #AthleteTurnedEntrepreneur #MindsetMastery
#HighPerformance #LeadershipDevelopment #ContentCreation
#BusinessStrategy

Introduction

Dre Baldwin is a former NBA basketball star who has transitioned from the court to the boardroom, impacting over 100 million entrepreneurs worldwide. Baldwin, who played professional basketball in the US and eight other countries, has since become a prolific author and motivational speaker. His Miami-based Company, Work On Your Game, is dedicated to helping high-level professionals and entrepreneurs achieve peak performance and results.

Humble Beginnings

Baldwin's journey began in Philadelphia, where he grew up playing various sports before settling on basketball. Despite a modest start, playing only one year of high school basketball and walking on to a Division III college team, Baldwin's determination saw him hustle his way into a professional career. Reflecting on his early days, Baldwin shared, "I only played one year of scholastic high school ball, walked on and played Division III college ball, which is the third lowest tier of college basketball. Hustled my way into playing pro basketball."

The Power of Mindset

A pivotal moment in Baldwin's career came when he started publishing videos on YouTube in 2005. Initially, these videos were for personal use, but they quickly garnered attention from aspiring athletes. This led Baldwin to explore the concept of mindset, which became the foundation of his Work On Your Game framework. "Mindset is about your consistent and habitual ways of thinking, your thought patterns, your ideas, your beliefs, and your attitudes," Baldwin explained. He emphasised that changing one's mindset involves conditioning and developing new habits through consistent practice.

Building a Brand Through Content

Baldwin's foray into content creation began with YouTube videos, which he posted sporadically until 2009. The turning point came when Google acquired YouTube and began monetising content. Baldwin realised the potential of this platform and started posting videos daily, writing articles, and creating training programmes for basketball players. "I realised, okay, there's an audience of people who want to see what a high-level player does every day in practice," Baldwin said. This strategic approach to content creation laid the groundwork for his brand.

The Transition to Writing

In addition to videos, Baldwin has authored 35 books, covering topics from mindset to professional basketball. His first book, *Buy a Game*, was a narrative of his basketball journey, aimed at his growing audience. Baldwin's writing process is hands-on, with every word penned by him. "Every word that comes out of Work On Your Game is written by me, always will be," he asserted. The advent of self-publishing allowed Baldwin to bypass traditional gatekeepers and share his insights directly with his audience.

The Work On Your Game University

Baldwin's latest venture, Work On Your Game University, offers high-level coaching, consulting, and speaking engagements. The university operates online, providing accessible education based on Baldwin's four-part framework: mindset, strategy, systems, and accountability. "The goal is to help you bring in more money in your business because we're working with entrepreneurs, and an entrepreneur's number one mandate is increasing value for shareholders," Baldwin noted.

Lessons in Marketing and Brand Building

Baldwin's success is a testament to the power of strategic marketing and brand building. He identified three key ways to draw attention: advertising, collaboration, and content. Advertising, while costly, produces quick results. Collaboration, such as guest appearances and joint ventures, allows for audience cross-pollination without any loss to either party. Content creation, though slow to yield results, is cost-effective and can be produced in large quantities. "Advertising, collaboration, content, and every entrepreneur, every marketer should be doing a mix of all three," Baldwin advised.

Overcoming Failures

Despite his success, Baldwin has faced numerous setbacks. He candidly shared that many of his products did not sell well, if at all. However, he views these failures as opportunities for future success. "I've created probably in my lifetime; I've probably created 500 different products... How many of them actually worked? I would say 10%, maybe," Baldwin revealed. He believes in the potential to reposition and market these products effectively in the future. "I'm not going to say any of them is dead because who knows, they might come back."

Conclusion

Dre Baldwin's journey from a professional athlete to a successful entrepreneur underscores the importance of mindset, strategic content creation, and resilience in the face of failure.

His approach to marketing – combining advertising, collaboration, and content – offers a comprehensive strategy for entrepreneurs seeking to get noticed.

"I became a professional athlete even though my start was very humble beginnings. It's mostly just about you having the right mindset, applying the right strategy, having the right working systems and then the accountability to make sure that everyone is doing their jobs."

SCAN TO LISTEN

 DRE BALDWIN

Chapter Forty-Two
Vegan Mission.

Vikas Garg
Founder and CEO, aBillion, Singapore

"Is it not possible to build algorithms to spread peace and positivity, and social impact, and benefit for society?"

Connecting Vegans of the World

#VikasGarg #abillion #SustainableLiving #VeganCommunity #EcoFriendly #DigitalImpact #GlobalSustainability #PlantBased #GreenTech #SocialEntrepreneurship

Introduction

Former banker Vikas Garg has embarked on a mission to make vegan dining and products easy to find. As the founder and CEO of aBillion, Singapore-based Garg has grown the platform into a global community, with its app downloaded in over 183 countries and more than 110,000 restaurants enrolled, and merchants of vegan products enrolled. This is a story of building a worldwide solution to local problems, which has massive marketing challenges to overcome.

The Genesis of aBillion

Vikas Garg's passion for animal rights and the environment has been a lifelong commitment, which naturally led him to a vegetarian and eventually vegan lifestyle. "We really started this company to help make that journey a lot easier and more accessible and more fun for a lot of people," Garg explains. The idea was to create a platform that would simplify the choices for consumers interested in plant-based diets and sustainable consumption.

Tackling the Chicken-and-Egg Problem

One of the most significant challenges for any user-generated content platform is the chicken-and-egg problem: how to attract users without existing content and vice versa. Garg candidly admits, "It's really hard work. If you looked at my first growth model back in 2017 or 18, those numbers, let's just say we're far off from those numbers."

To overcome this, Garg employed a mix of common sense and innovative strategies. Initially, he tried traditional marketing methods like Google and Facebook ads, but these yielded only a small trickle of users. The breakthrough came when he started engaging with influencers and animal sanctuaries. "We started talking to influencers and all these people who are like on Instagram and incredibly passionate about the environment and about animals," he recalls.

Gamification and Altruism

A pivotal moment in aBillion's growth was the introduction of gamification and altruism into the platform. Instead of spending money on ads, Garg decided to reward users for their reviews with credits that could be donated to various causes. "We gave everybody a dollar of cash. When they post a review, they can't withdraw that money. They can't go and buy something. They can choose where aBillion as a company donates that dollar," Garg explains.

This strategy not only incentivised user engagement but also aligned with the company's core values. Today, aBillion has nearly 100 nonprofits in its coalition and is close to donating $3 million to various causes, including animal sanctuaries, feeding hungry children, and planting trees.

Building a Sustainable Revenue Model

While the altruistic approach helped build a community, sustaining the business required a robust revenue model. aBillion has developed a SaaS product that 5,000 of its 217,000 companies use, generating a steady stream of income. Additionally, the platform features a consumer marketplace where aBillion takes a small percentage of each transaction. "We receive 10%. We receive a small portion of every transaction," Garg notes.

Leveraging Search Engine Optimisation for Organic Growth

One of the most ingenious aspects of aBillion's growth strategy is its reliance on organic search engine optimisation (SEO). Early on, Garg and his team built a mobile-responsive website that functioned like an app. This decision paid off in spades. "On any given day, if you were to Google one of them, or if you were to Google, especially for the consumer products brands, if you were to Google one of their products, there's a one in three chance that our website shows up on page one of Google results," Garg reveals.

This organic visibility has been a significant driver of growth, attracting two to three companies daily to claim their businesses on aBillion without any marketing spend.

The Importance of Purpose

For Garg, the key to enduring the challenges of entrepreneurship lies in finding purpose. "If you can find purpose, and if you can find something to do as an entrepreneur that allows you to connect your values and sort of your purpose in life to your work, you will work harder on it through the hard times, through the good times, through the hard times," he advises.

This sense of purpose has not only kept Garg motivated but has also resonated with the community he has built. "If aBillion succeeds, it solves something for me and my own identity in this world," he adds.

Conclusion

Vikas Garg's journey with aBillion offers a masterclass in building a community-driven platform. By leveraging gamification, altruism, and SEO, he has created a sustainable business that aligns with his values. For entrepreneurs, the key take away is clear: find your purpose, and let it guide your marketing strategy.

"Show up every day, be present, and if you really believe in something, go for it."

SCAN TO LISTEN

 VIKAS GARG

Chapter Forty-Three
Trial and Learn.

Allison "Ali" M. Wing

CEO + Board Member + Advisor + Impact Investor, Oobli, Davis, California, USA

"Getting to simplicity is our single hardest problem but the most important solution."

Marketing the World a Sweeter Place, Without Sugar

#Oobli #SugarRevolution #Biotech #HealthyEating
#SustainableSolutions #FoodInnovation #SweetProtein
#DiabetesPrevention #ObesityAwareness #EcoFriendlyFood

Introduction

In a world where 75% of all food contains sugar, the battle against obesity and diabetes is more critical than ever. Enter Ali Wing, CEO of Oobli, a biotechnology company pioneering the use of sweet proteins to offer a healthier alternative to sugar. Based in the USA, Ali Wing brings a wealth of experience in consumer marketing to her role, aiming to revolutionise how we perceive and consume sweetness.

The Sweet Protein Revolution

Oobli's mission is nothing short of revolutionary. The company has developed the world's first sweet protein product, a breakthrough that could significantly impact global health. "Sweet proteins are the first time we've ever had available in the world, let alone in any way in our food system, a protein pathway to giving us our sweet tooth rather than a carbohydrate pathway," explains Wing.

Sweet proteins, derived from plants and berries that evolved along the equator, trick our taste buds into thinking we've consumed sugar. However, unlike carbohydrates, these proteins do not interact with our blood sugar system or gut microbiome. This fundamental difference could be a game changer in addressing obesity and diabetes.

The Marriage of Nature and Technology

The journey to bring sweet proteins to market has been long and arduous, involving eight years of research and development. "This is the perfect marriage of the best of nature and the best of technology," says Wing. By leveraging advances in biotechnology and fermentation, Oobli can produce these proteins in a climate-friendly, scalable, and affordable way.

The environmental benefits are also significant. A mere 1% reduction in sugar production could save 650,000 acres of land. "Sugar is actually a really important thing, kind of like fossil fuel. We just need to use it differently," notes Wing.

Overcoming Industry Challenges

Introducing a new product in an entrenched industry is no small feat. The sugar industry is well-established, and consumer behaviour is deeply ingrained. "I'm not trying to disrupt an industry. I'm actually trying to solve a crisis," says Wing. The crisis she refers to is the global epidemic of obesity and diabetes.

To change consumer behaviour, Oobli focuses on making their products as craveable as possible. "We start and stop with the consumer," Wing emphasises. The goal is to offer foods that are as good for our bodies as they are for our souls, without asking consumers to compromise on taste.

Marketing Strategies: Trial and Education

One of the most effective ways to introduce a new product is through trial and sampling. Oobli launched its first sweet protein-powered products in mid-June, focusing on digital education and physical sampling. "We sampled more than 15,000 teas in the months of July and August," shares Wing. The company targeted early adopters and innovators, showing up at culturally relevant locations like movie nights and popular hiking spots in Los Angeles.

Oobli also leverages online sampling. "We are creating several campaigns where if you take the time to go listen to Dr. Jason

Ryder, our chief technology officer, we send you a free six-pack," explains Wing. This approach not only educates consumers but also encourages them to try the product. Oobli is focused on education, with experts brought on as strategic advisers, providing the content for consumers to learn more about the science behind the pea protein innovation.

Wing underscores the importance of measurement. "Understand and design systems of measurement to understand, make sure you know what you learned," she says. This approach ensures that mistakes are not repeated and that the company continually improves.

The Importance of Taste

For consumers, ultimately it will be the flavour that they buy. "We are not trying to tell a consumer what to taste. We're asking them, what's your favourite drink that we're going to target and replace?" says Wing. The company aims to reformulate popular products so that four out of five consumers can't notice a difference. This strategy ensures that consumers don't have to make a change; they get the same taste they love but in a healthier form.

Learning from Mistakes

Even the best-laid plans can go awry. Wing candidly shares a significant mistake Oobli made during their initial product launch. "We were so excited about bringing out this craveable sweet tea that had 75% less sugar, we didn't pay enough attention to how protein was going to show up on the nutrition fact panel," she admits. The result was a label that incorrectly indicated zero protein, confusing consumers.

The company quickly corrected the mistake, redesigning the packaging to include an asterisk and an explanation. "That's a great example of fail fast, admit it, and adjust," says Wing.

Conclusion

For entrepreneurs, the key take away is clear: engage the consumer, avoid the illusion of perfection, and always measure your progress.

"Fail fast. Don't be afraid to be in market and learn," Ali advises. "There is no such thing as perfection. All we can do is build, be smart, and agile."

SCAN TO LISTEN

 # ALI
WING

Chapter Forty-Four
Beer Time.

Mark Wong
IMPOSSIBREW®, London, UK

"It's one of those once in a lifetime experiences. And so I thought, might as well."

The Dragons' Den Drink

#Impossibrew #NonAlcoholicBeer #SoberCurious #HealthierChoices #Nootropics #BeerInnovation #AlcoholFree #CraftBeerRevolution #MindfulDrinking #SustainableBrewing

Introduction

Getting a free public launch on TV is a dream for any publicity agent. Mark Wong, the founder of IMPOSSIBREW®, achieved this when he was invited onto Dragons' Den just a few weeks into his university side hustle. Although they didn't secure an investor from their appearance on the show, Wong and his young team saw explosive sales. Building a brand in any category is challenging, but in the fast-moving consumer goods market, where advertising budgets and distribution are key, growing a new brand demands all the academic rigour and business acumen of this Hong Kong-born, UK-educated entrepreneur.

Mission IMPOSSIBREW®

Mark Wong's passion for beer began at a young age. "Ever since I was young, anything I could see that, well, I knew if you could brew a beer or make a cocktail, you'd get invited to parties at school," he recalls. However, a health scare in his early 20s forced him to reconsider his drinking habits. This led to the inception of IMPOSSIBREW®, a brand that aims to offer the social benefits of beer without the downsides of alcohol.

Understanding the Market

Wong's approach to the no- and low-alcohol market is rooted in a deep understanding of consumer behaviour. "We do consume drinks that change our mental state," he explains. "In the morning, we would wake up either with a coffee or some people have an energy drink or a tea, that picks you up. And in the evening, there is the element of evening relaxation. And that typically is alcohol."

IMPOSSIBREW® leverages nootropics – natural substances that enhance cognitive function – to replicate the relaxing effects of alcohol. "The goal of what we're trying to deliver is that slight sense of one or two-pint feeling, that slight sort of relaxation when you're having a chat with friends," says Wong.

The Power of Direct-to-Consumer Sales

One of the most striking aspects of IMPOSSIBREW®'s strategy is its focus on direct-to-consumer sales. "We thought that I didn't like carrying 10, 20 beers from a supermarket to bring it into my flat," Wong notes. By selling directly through their website, IMPOSSIBREW® maintains a direct relationship with its customers, allowing for immediate feedback and rapid iteration of their products.

Leveraging Social Media

Social media has been a cornerstone of IMPOSSIBREW®'s marketing strategy. Wong and his team have harnessed the power of platforms like Instagram and TikTok to document their entrepreneurial journey in real time. "We started doing sort of really dynamic videos on Instagram and TikTok. It was just essentially just fully about the startup journey," he explains.

This approach has resonated with audiences, as evidenced by their substantial followings – 35,000 on Instagram and 65,500 on TikTok. "On TikTok, people are looking to be entertained and to be inspired and to see what life is like in a way that isn't something people already know," Wong adds.

The Dragons' Den Experience

Appearing on Dragons' Den was a pivotal moment for IMPOSSIBREW®, even though they did not secure investment. "The questions were really difficult. They were hard, but at least I think the session went well," Wong reflects. The exposure from the show led to a significant spike in sales, demonstrating the power of media relations in boosting brand visibility.

Learning from Mistakes

Wong is candid about the mistakes made along the way. One notable error was spending 90% of their initial budget on a branding agency that did not deliver the desired results. "It just didn't come up the way that we wanted it to. And we didn't have any more money for revisions," he admits. This experience taught him the importance of clear communication and alignment with external partners.

Customer Engagement

A key element of IMPOSSIBREW®'s success has been its focus on customer engagement. Wong personally called early customers to gather feedback, which informed product improvements and marketing strategies. "It's almost in a weird way, like a community effort that I could just pick up the phone and the customer would be like, 'Oh, what do you think about this one?' And the people are really nice and they're happy to help," he says.

Conclusion

Mark Wong's ambition to take on the large and competitive beer market with a nootropics-based drink is full of lessons. Their focus on building genuine relationships with customers, a willingness to adapt based on customer feedback, and a social media-led marketing campaign have kept them in business. An early spot on Dragons' Den was a good boost but didn't translate into investment. Ultimately, a business survives on customers.

As Wong puts it, "Listening to our customers has definitely shaped us into where we are today."

SCAN TO LISTEN

 MARK WONG

Chapter Forty-Five
AI Nuptials.

Chris Troka
Owner, Focused-Biz & Wedding DJ, Milwaukee, Wisconsin, USA

"If you could take that collective knowledge and put that into a ChatBot, what would that do for your customer service experience?"

Making Money as the Wedding DJ

#WeddingDJ #EntrepreneurJourney #InnovativeDJ #EventPlanning #DigitalMarketing #WeddingPlanning #DJLife #TechSavvyDJ #AIChatbot #NicheMarketing

Introduction

The Wedding Singer, My Big Fat Greek Wedding, The Wedding Planner, Four Weddings and a Funeral, The Wedding Date... weddings are an endless source of entertainment, and there is money to be made providing it. Located on the shores of Lake Michigan, Chris Troka has built a profitable business in the wedding industry with his company, MUP DJs. His journey from a nine-to-five job to becoming an award-winning wedding DJ service provider includes insights on niching down and also the use of AI for customer service.

The Journey to Specialisation

Chris Troka's foray into the DJ business began with a simple desire to escape the monotony of a traditional job. "I always wanted to own a business and I knew I had to do something about it," he recalls. Initially, he started DJing for parties and anniversaries, avoiding weddings due to their perceived complexity. However, a single wedding gig changed his perspective. "I tried one wedding and we actually turned out to be pretty fantastic at it. So, I realised I only want to do weddings now."

This shift in focus allowed Troka to hone his skills and become an expert in the wedding DJ niche. "A DJ actually is kind of like a wedding planner, in a sense, where they help keep the timeline moving," he explains. By specialising, Troka was able to offer a more tailored and professional service, which in turn attracted more clients.

Leveraging Technology for Efficiency

One of the key strategies that propelled MUP DJs to success was the adoption of technology to streamline operations. Troka's background in digital marketing played a crucial role in this transformation. "I had some experience in running digital ads.

So working together, they introduced me to ideas and tools," he says, referring to his time at a marketing agency.

Troka implemented a three-step portal system that mimics a marketing funnel. This system includes a DJ Quote Building tool, a digital contract form, and a CRM to nurture leads with personalised email touchpoints. "We realised, wow, people don't have printers and not everyone has checks anymore. So we needed to get with the times," he notes. This automation not only improved efficiency but also enhanced the customer experience by removing friction from the buying journey.

The Role of Content Marketing

Content marketing has been another cornerstone of Troka's strategy. Inspired by HubSpot's inbound marketing principles, he focused on creating valuable content for potential clients. "We saw the importance of blogging. This isn't just good for your keywords and your SEO, but these can be great resources and articles that help move people from a slightly cold lead into a warm lead into a very interested buyer," Troka explains.

By offering informative blogs on topics like wedding DJ pricing and typical wedding games, Troka positioned MUP DJs as a trusted advisor in the wedding industry. "Whether they booked with our DJ service or not, I'd rather provide that information for them so you can have a great wedding. It's not about booking with us. It's about providing value," he emphasises.

Embracing AI for Customer Engagement

In a bid to further enhance customer engagement, Troka integrated an AI-powered chatbot into his website. This chatbot, powered by ChatGPT, offers instant responses to common queries, significantly improving the speed to lead. "Buyers nowadays are researching on their own. They're looking to kind of find out more information and make an informed decision," Troka says.

The chatbot's ability to provide personalised music recommendations and answer planning questions has been a game changer. "Chatbots are a great way to make yourself accessible as a business," Troka notes. This innovation not only saves time but also ensures that potential clients receive timely and accurate information.

Building Strong Relationships

While technology and content marketing have been pivotal, Troka also underscores the importance of building strong relationships. "We decided to begin nurturing and building relationships with other venues in the area," he says. This network of partnerships has become an unofficial sales force, constantly referring new clients to MUP DJs.

Customer service is another area where Troka excels. "We wanted our customer service to be so on point that couples just raved about us," he explains. This focus on exceptional service has resulted in numerous five-star reviews and repeat business, even for second and third weddings.

Conclusion

Troka's journey hasn't been without its challenges. One of the key lessons he shares is the importance of seizing opportunities. "You have to strike while the iron is hot. If you see an opportunity and you feel excited about it, you must go for it," he advises.

However, he also cautions against expanding without sufficient resources.

"Try and make sure you get some money from a customer in advance, because you can solve any problem if you've got cash."

SCAN TO LISTEN

 CHRIS TROKA

Chapter Forty-Six
Art Consumption.

Hussein Hallak
Founder and CEO, Momentable, Vancouver, Canada

"Continuing that constant conversation with our audience is a core tenet of how we market and how we bring the community along with us."

Unlocking the Vaults of the Art World

#ArtTech #DigitalArtPlatform #CulturalDemocratization
#InnovativeArt #ArtForAll #TechInArt #ArtWorldRevolution
#MomentableArt #NFT #BlockChain

Introduction

In his adopted home of Vancouver, Canada, Hussein Hallak loves art. With over 20 years of experience running his own businesses, Hallak has embarked on a mission to make art available to everyone through his latest venture, Momentable.art. This innovative platform aims to bring art into homes, akin to a "Spotify for art," but also offers artists a way to monetise their works via non-fungible tokens (NFTs).

The Vision Behind Momentable.art

Hussein Hallak's passion for art traces back to his childhood in Damascus, Syria. He recalls a vivid memory of a painting in his family's sitting room that sparked conversations and left a lasting impression on him. "For many, the art world seems distant, locked away, hidden, only accessible for people who have money or have the time," Hallak explains.

Overall percentages paint an even more dramatic picture. The Tate shows about 20% of its permanent collection. The Louvre shows 8%, the Guggenheim a lowly 3%, and the Berlinische Galerie – a Berlin museum whose mandate is to show, preserve, and collect art made in the city – 2% of its holdings.

Momentable.art seeks to bridge this gap by providing the best visual experience of art to customers through software.

The platform's latest release, Momentable DaVinci, exemplifies this vision. It offers a high-resolution, immersive experience of art, allowing users to explore and appreciate masterpieces from the comfort of their homes. "We wanted to create something similar without technology coming in the way," Hallak notes, emphasising the importance of an unobstructed art experience.

Solving the Art Accessibility Problem

One of the significant challenges Hallak identified is the fragmented nature of art accessibility. Artworks are often scattered across various platforms, making it difficult for enthusiasts to piece together a cohesive experience. "The best experience of art and the most honest experience is being in front of the painting," Hallak asserts. Momentable.art aims to replicate this by offering a seamless, uninterrupted journey through art history.

The platform also incorporates personalisation features, similar to those found on Spotify or Netflix. "The more you like and interact with things, the more it shows you something close to this," Hallak explains. This approach caters to individual tastes, helping users discover art that resonates with them, even if they lack formal knowledge of art genres.

Empowering Contemporary Artists

Momentable.art is not just about showcasing historical art; it also provides a platform for contemporary artists to exhibit and monetise their work. Hallak observed that most artists rely on a single income stream – selling their paintings. This model is fraught with challenges, as unsold paintings translate to financial instability. "An artist, if they sell a painting, they survive. If they don't, they starve," Hallak remarks.

To address this, Momentable.art offers artists their own channels within the platform, where they can display digital versions of their work. These channels can be monetised through subscriptions, tips, and donations. "We said, give us your digital files. We put them on the platform. The platform organises them," Hallak explains. This model provides artists with a continuous revenue stream and a broader audience reach.

Leveraging Blockchain Technology

Hallak is a strong proponent of NFT technology, which he believes can revolutionise the art world. "The NFT technology allows the transfer of ownership in digital form, which never existed before," he states. By integrating blockchain, Momentable.art ensures that artists receive royalties from the sale of their digital art in perpetuity. This feature addresses a long-standing issue in the art market, where artists often lose control over their work once it is sold.

Marketing Strategies and Community Engagement

Building a successful SaaS product like Momentable.art requires more than just a great idea; it demands effective marketing strategies. Hallak emphasises the importance of being product-led in marketing efforts. "The product has to provide the experience that we promised," he asserts. This principle guides their marketing campaigns, such as the Da Vinci month, where they promote the platform through the lens of Da Vinci's life and works.

Another cornerstone of Momentable.art's marketing strategy is community engagement. The platform hosts events on Discord, attracting a vibrant community of art enthusiasts. "We hold fun events where people go experience the platform, play around with it," Hallak shares. These events foster a sense of belonging and encourage users to explore and share their experiences.

Hallak also highlights the importance of maintaining a constant conversation with the community. "Share, even if you say good morning, if you say, hi, I'm working on this, you know,

I'm struggling with this," he advises. This approach keeps the community engaged and invested in the platform's journey.

Lessons from Past Mistakes

As a seasoned entrepreneur, Hallak has had his share of missteps. One significant lesson he shares is the importance of continuous engagement with the community. "Assuming that the community only wants to hear from me when I have something valuable to share" was a mistake, he admits. Regular updates, even about small progress or challenges, help maintain a connection with the audience.

Team Alignment and Collective Ownership

Hallak underscores the value of team alignment in driving a company's success. "Everybody's job is to make the company successful. Everybody's job is marketing. Everybody's job is making the product great," he asserts. By involving the entire team in marketing discussions and setting clear goals, Momentable.art has seen significant improvements in performance and morale.

Conclusion

Hussein Hallak's journey with Momentable.art offers valuable insights for entrepreneurs seeking to get their businesses noticed. From leveraging technology to empower artists to maintaining constant community engagement, Hallak's strategies are both innovative and effective.

For all of these attributes, he highlights the importance of communication,

"Maintaining a conversation is a core element of an entrepreneur's journey."

SCAN TO LISTEN

 HUSSEIN

HALLAK

Chapter Forty-Seven
Niche Runway.

Roberto Capodieci
Chief Technology Officer, SimFly, Bali, Singapore

"The community grows around a common interest. So that's the channel to get to a lot of people."

A Community of Virtual Pilots

#BlockchainTechnology #FlightSimulator #Blockchain
#DigitalInnovation #SimFly #CryptoGaming #NFTs
#TechEntrepreneur #BlockchainGaming #StartupSuccess

Introduction

Far away from overhead flight paths, Bali-based Roberto Capodieci is one of the captains of a virtual business in the sky. As the Chief Technology Officer at SimFly, Capodieci was brought into the Singapore registered company to help expand the flight simulator business. There is literally a whole industry which exists only in the virtual domain, and which is generating healthy profits. The marketing challenges have included overcoming the distrust about non-fungible tokens (NFTs) and how to reach people who are in the air.

The Power of Niching

Capodieci's story begins with an unexpected revelation about the power of niching. "If you're running a business and you're not sure that niching is the right thing to do, then today's insights are definitely for you," he asserts. SimFly targets a specific audience: enthusiasts of flight simulation. This niche, while seemingly narrow, is both passionate and willing to invest in their hobby.

"Microsoft themselves have celebrated 10 million active users in the world of flight simulators," Capodieci notes. This statistic underscores the potential of targeting a niche market. By focusing on a specific interest, SimFly has tapped into a community that is not only large but also deeply engaged.

Building Trust in a Sceptical Market

One of the significant challenges Capodieci faced was building trust within the flight simulation community, especially when introducing blockchain technology. "As soon as people heard NFT tokens, blockchain, the reaction was very mixed," he recalls. The initial scepticism was palpable, with some even labelling the venture as a scam.

To overcome this, Capodieci emphasised transparency and education. "We had to build trust. We had to show that we are there for real, that we are working hard and we deliver," he explains. By addressing concerns head-on and demonstrating the value of blockchain in ensuring the singularity of digital assets, SimFly gradually won over the community.

Leveraging Social Media and Influencers

Capodieci also highlights the importance of social media and influencers in modern marketing. "YouTubers are a perfect channel to promote something," he states. By collaborating with influencers who have a dedicated following within the flight simulation niche, SimFly was able to reach a highly targeted audience.

"People that go to a niche, they have less followers, they're cheaper, but those followers listen to them much more attentively," Capodieci explains. This strategy not only proved cost-effective but also highly impactful, as niche influencers often have a more engaged and loyal audience.

The Role of Community Engagement

Community engagement has been a cornerstone of SimFly's success. Capodieci underscores the importance of showing appreciation and rewarding loyal customers. "It's important to build the core of this community, this client base," he says. By fostering a sense of belonging and actively involving users in the development process, SimFly has created a robust and supportive community.

Capodieci also advises entrepreneurs to be present on multiple platforms to reach different segments of their audience. "We have a nice channel in Discord, we have a newsletter, we have other means," he shares. This multichannel approach ensures that SimFly can engage with users wherever they are most comfortable.

Lessons in Marketing and Brand Building

Reflecting on his journey, Capodieci offers several key lessons for entrepreneurs. One of the most crucial is the importance of consistency in marketing efforts. "Never enter a channel that you cannot afford the continuity of," he advises. Marketing is not a one-off effort but a continuous process that requires patience and persistence.

He also stresses the value of seeking expert advice. "If somebody is a one-man show, I suggest going to a consultant. Those are money well spent," he recommends. Recognising the limits of one's expertise and investing in professional guidance can save time and resources in the long run.

Conclusion

SimFly offers insights into the power of niching, building trust, leveraging social media, and engaging with the community. Capodieci's insights are examples of the potential of targeted marketing and the importance of consistency and expert advice.

"Sometimes having a big effect on a little amount of people is better than to have a little effect on a big quantity of people."

SCAN TO LISTEN

 ROBERTO CAPODIECI

Chapter Forty-Eight
Franchise Development.

John Prothro

President and CEO, Foot Solutions, Inc., Atlanta, Georgia, USA

"The value proposition has to be brought into the conversation very early."

Customers Walk Away Smiling

#FranchiseSuccess #FootSolutions #Orthotics #HealthcareInnovation #GlobalFranchising #Biomechanics #RetailTechnology #EntrepreneurLife #WellnessIndustry #BusinessStrategy

Introduction

After an international career in mergers and acquisitions, John Prothro is living in Alpharetta, Georgia, acting as President and CEO of Foot Solutions. The company is revolutionising the foot wellness industry with a combination of technology, brand, and sponsorship of pickleball tournaments!

The Genesis of Foot Solutions

Foot Solutions is not just a retailer; it is a sanctuary for those suffering from foot ailments. With around 80 locations globally, the company offers custom orthotics and healthy footwear, addressing issues from plantar fasciitis to diabetic foot problems. "We are a foot wellness retailer. We sell custom orthotics and healthy footwear, but the reason you go to Foot Solutions is because you have a problem," says Prothro.

Embracing Technology for Better Solutions

One of the key differentiators for Foot Solutions is its use of advanced technology. The company employs a sophisticated CAD CAM software and 3D printing to create custom orthotics. "The way that most companies are building custom orthotics is the same way they were building them 50 years ago. We figured there was a better way to do it," Prothro explains. This modern approach not only enhances the quality of the product but also sets Foot Solutions apart in a crowded market.

Building a Global Franchise

Prothro's experience in M&A has been instrumental in expanding Foot Solutions. After acquiring the company, he focused on buying franchise locations from retiring owners and integrating new technology. "We bought up some franchise locations, a couple of technology elements, and another company called Happy Feet Plus. Now, we're building out new franchises and selling them," he shares.

The Importance of a Robust System

For Prothro, the success of a franchise lies in its system. "The system needs to be clean and airtight. You've got to have a playbook that you could hand to someone else, a reasonably competent person that you could train," he advises. This structured approach ensures that each franchise operates efficiently and maintains the brand's high standards.

Differentiation and Barriers to Entry

In a market teeming with competitors, differentiation is crucial. Prothro emphasises the importance of having a unique selling proposition. "You need to have something that's special about what you're doing. If someone can do something very similar right down the street, there's a greater risk profile," he notes. For Foot Solutions, this differentiation comes from their advanced technology and highly trained staff.

Marketing and Brand Building

Marketing is a multifaceted endeavour for Foot Solutions. The company has its own internal marketing agency, focusing on digital ad buys, Google AdWords, and traditional advertising where appropriate. "We have our own internal agency. We tried external agencies but didn't like the results. Now, we have people focused full-time on our company," Prothro explains.

The company also employs a hub-and-spoke model to build brand awareness regionally. Sponsorships play a significant role in their strategy. "We sponsor the Pro Pickleball Association. It's the fastest-growing sport in the world. We wear our Foot Solutions shirts at events, which helps in brand building," he adds.

Their message is clear, "Your feet are the foundation of your health. Let us take care of them for you."

Lessons from Mistakes

Prothro is candid about the lessons learned from past mistakes, particularly in marketing. "Agencies can bring more people to a problem, but if it becomes sort of a lower person who's basically just an outsource hire, it's not effective. We decided to build our own internal team," he reveals. This shift has allowed Foot Solutions to have a more focused and knowledgeable marketing team.

Conclusion

Beyond the business strategies and technological advancements, Prothro underscores the importance of personal fulfilment and balance.

"If you focus entirely on making money, you might find yourself waking up having accomplished your goal but being entirely unsuccessful with the rest of your life."

SCAN TO LISTEN

 JOHN

PROTHRO

Chapter Forty-Nine
Entrepreneur Mindset.

Annie Margarita Yang
Best-Selling Author, The 5-Day Job Searc

"The goal is to write a book so that you position yourself as an authority and open up opportunities for yourself."

Don't Worry About the Nos, Only the Yes Matters

#SelfMadeEntrepreneur #FinancialFreedom #AnnieYangFinancial #PersonalBranding #FinancialLiteracy #EntrepreneurMindset #BookAsBusinessCard #DigitalMarketing #InnovativeEntrepreneur #CareerDevelopment

Introduction

Annie Margarita Yang grew disillusioned with the financial advice that her generation was receiving and set out to change the narrative. Based in Boston, she initially believed that joining an accounting firm was the right path. However, lacking an accounting degree, she faced the harsh realities of recruitment. Turning obstacles into opportunities, she founded Annie Yang Financial, a firm dedicated to providing practical advice to a growing community of young people.

A Desire to Help

Annie's aspiration to help people with their finances began at the age of 20. Despite her initial foray into communications, her true passion lay in financial advisory. "I always knew that I wanted to help people with their finances," she explains. "But I just didn't know how because a lot of jobs in finance are more about selling stocks and mutual funds rather than genuinely helping people manage their money."

Her determination to break into the finance industry led her to pursue a degree in communications, a strategic move to "check the box" and gain credibility in the job market. "People weren't interested in talking to me or giving me an opportunity without a degree," she recalls. "So, I got a communications degree because it was quicker and easier than an accounting degree."

Leveraging Authorship for Career Advancement

Annie's innovative approach to standing out in the job market involved writing a book. Attending a high-pressure sales pitch at a small business expo, she was inspired to author *1001 Ways to Save Money*. This book became a pivotal tool in her career advancement.

"I put 'author of *1001 Ways to Save Money*' right under the education line on my resume," she says. "People were calling me left and right to give me an interview."

From Career to Entrepreneur

Annie secured herself a job and then often asked potential recruits to describe the hardest problem they have ever faced and how they solved it, a question that provides deep insights into their capabilities.

"80% of the answers came back as the hardest problem they ever had was that they were fired or laid off, and they couldn't get a job quickly," she notes. This insight led her to write *The 5-Day Job Search*, addressing a common challenge faced by many job seekers.

The Role of AI in Marketing

She used ChatGPT to craft her Amazon product description and generate 50 sales and marketing funnel ideas. "The input is what is important," she emphasises. "I gave it 10 pieces of information, and it gave me an amazing product description that I hardly needed to edit."

This innovative use of AI not only streamlined her marketing processes but also allowed her to focus on implementing various strategies. "I decided to implement all 50 ideas from ChatGPT," she says. "By the time I'm done with all 50, this should be technically like an empire."

Yang also paid to try multiple AI image creators, which could be used by people to generate photographs for their resumes, without the costs of using a professional photographer. She then posted the full results on her blog.

She built a launch team by sending personal messages to 2,000 contacts asking them to purchase the new book. It became a number one release in the career category on Amazon and was ranked 88 across the entire Kindle free store.

Effective Marketing Strategies

One of Annie's most effective marketing strategies has been leveraging podcasts to promote her book. Recognising that podcast listeners are often interested in educational content, she set an ambitious goal to appear on 500 podcasts. "I realise now that's too big," she admits. "I'm actually getting burned out. But I've been booked on 125, and this is my 92nd one."

Her experience highlights the importance of setting realistic goals and the value of podcasts as a medium for reaching a targeted audience. Additionally, Annie's strategy of securing her username handles across all social media platforms, even if she isn't actively using them, demonstrates a proactive approach to brand protection.

Booking Her Handles on Social Media

Yang's approach to social media is both strategic and comprehensive. While she acknowledges the advice to focus on one platform, she has chosen to establish a presence across multiple channels, inspired by the practices of established figures like Tony Robbins and Marie Forleo.

"I decided to take up all of the username handles before anyone else could," she says. "Even if my Facebook has only 21 followers, it's about securing the digital real estate."

Overcoming Challenges

Despite her successes, Annie has faced her share of challenges, particularly with YouTube. She has experienced what she believes to be shadow banning, where her subscriber count fluctuates inexplicably, likely due to the platform's algorithmic biases.

"Every time I hit 18,300 subscribers, I would lose 20 or 30, and then gain them back again," she laments. "It's clear that YouTube's algorithm prioritises mainstream media over independent creators."

This experience highlights the importance of diversifying one's online presence and not relying too heavily on a single platform. It also underscores the need for entrepreneurs to stay adaptable and resilient in the face of digital challenges.

Learning from Mistakes

Yang candidly shares one of her biggest marketing oversights: not building an email list from the start. "In my four years of making YouTube videos, I never bothered to get people onto my email list," she confesses. "Now that I've gotten shadow banned, I realise it would have been nice to have people on my email list."

Conclusion

Annie Margarita Yang's story is a compelling example of how persistence can lead to remarkable success. Just as she wished for, she has become a trusted source of financial advice to the younger generation, without hype or sales.

Yang summed her philosophy to getting noticed. "Go big or go home."

SCAN TO LISTEN

 ANNIE
YANG

Chapter Fifty
Revitalising a Legacy Brand.

Joe Hart
President/CEO, Dale Carnegie & Associates, Co-Author of Take Command, New York, New York, USA

"People support a world they help create."

The Mission of a Business Leader with a Vision

#DaleCarnegie #Leadership #PersonalDevelopment #GlobalStrategy #Innovation #ChangeManagement #DigitalTransformation #SoftSkills #JoeHart #CorporateTraining

Introduction

In motor city USA, Detroit, Michigan, Joe Hart, the global CEO of Dale Carnegie, has been at the helm of one of the most iconic names in management theory. Dale Carnegie, a name synonymous with self-improvement and business acumen, has touched millions of lives worldwide. Hart's leadership of the company, which began in 2015, provides a case study of the power of listening, brand rejuvenation, and strategic vision. This is an example of having an entrepreneurial vision and leadership style, even when running a large and established corporation.

A Legacy Reimagined

Founded in 1912 by Dale Carnegie, the company has grown to operate in 86 countries with 200 operations. Despite its age, the brand remains a cornerstone in the realm of personal and professional development. Hart's mission has been to modernise and revitalise this venerable institution.

"Dale Carnegie's principles are timeless, but the way we deliver them must evolve," Hart explains. "We needed to modernise the brand, make it more relevant for today's audience."

Listening as a Leadership Strategy

Upon taking the reins, Hart faced the challenge of steering a well-established organisation towards a new vision. His approach was rooted in one of Dale Carnegie's core teachings: the importance of listening.

"One of the biggest challenges I had was mobilising a company that had been successful around the imperative of really taking command of what we were doing," Hart recalls. "I spent a number of months really just listening and understanding."

Hart's listening tour was extensive. He travelled globally, meeting with franchisees and team members, both in person and via digital means. This approach not only built trust but also provided invaluable insights into the opportunities and challenges faced by the organisation.

Building a Foundation for Change

Hart's initial strategy, dubbed the "foundation strategy," focused on reactivating the brand and fostering a unified global team. This involved a comprehensive technology overhaul and a renewed emphasis on thought leadership and customer connection.

"We wanted to really activate the brand, modernising it and making it even more relevant for people," Hart says. "It was not just a global rebranding, but also about connecting with the customer and having research that we're conducting around the world."

The foundation strategy laid the groundwork for what Hart calls the "elevation strategy," aimed at propelling the company to new heights. This phased approach ensured that the changes were sustainable and well received by all stakeholders.

The Power of Authenticity

Hart's personal connection to Dale Carnegie's teachings has been a driving force in his leadership. As a young lawyer, he took a Dale Carnegie course that profoundly impacted his career trajectory, leading him to leave law and pursue business.

"I shared my story, the fact that I had left the practice of law because I was so influenced by what I've learned in Dale Carnegie," Hart shares. "People really want authenticity."

This authenticity was evident in his early interactions with franchisees. At a pivotal meeting in Chicago, Hart's emotional recounting of his journey with Dale Carnegie resonated deeply with the audience, building a foundation of trust and mutual respect.

Engaging a New Generation

Recognising the need to reach a younger audience, Hart has spearheaded initiatives to make Dale Carnegie's teachings accessible to a new generation. This includes the introduction of a new book, *Take Command*, which builds on Carnegie's principles while addressing contemporary challenges.

"*Take Command* is about taking command first of your thoughts and your emotions," Hart explains. "It's built on Dale Carnegie's ideas but deals with the kind of problems and challenges that people have in their lives today."

The book is designed to be engaging and relatable, with stories from diverse individuals around the world. It addresses issues such as imposter syndrome, the comparison trap, and the importance of building strong relationships.

Embracing Digital Transformation

In an era where digital consumption is the norm, Hart has ensured that Dale Carnegie's content is available in various formats. This includes short-form videos and other digital media aimed at younger audiences who may not be inclined to read long-form books.

"People do consume information very differently, particularly your daughters, my kids, that generation," Hart notes. "We are working on reaching them through various digital media, short-form videos, and other kinds of things."

This digital transformation was particularly crucial during the COVID-19 pandemic, which necessitated a swift pivot from in-person training to dynamic, interactive online training. This agility has positioned Dale Carnegie to emerge from the pandemic stronger and more competitive.

Lessons in Patience and Vision

Hart's journey has not been without its challenges. One of the key lessons he has learned is the importance of patience and realistic expectations.

"My hope had been to have inspired change faster at Dale Carnegie. It took longer than I thought," Hart admits. "Particularly when dealing with a larger organisation or just people and change, there is a foundation that has to happen."

Despite these challenges, Hart's unwavering commitment to his vision has been instrumental in driving the company's success. His advice to fellow entrepreneurs is to create a compelling vision that people can rally around.

"When we can create a compelling vision, when we can align other people, get people excited about it, and back that up by a commitment and action so that there's integrity, that's ultimately what it takes to move and to create something," Hart advises.

Conclusion

Joe Hart's leadership of Dale Carnegie provides useful lessons in updating a legacy brand while staying true to its core principles. Through listening, authenticity, and a clear vision, he has brought the organisation with him on the path of modernisation. He's also introduced digital technologies so that the company doesn't just think differently, it operates differently too. By writing his own book, faithful to the principles of Carnegie but updated for the current generation, Hart also very much led by example.

Hart sums up his approach.

"Dale Carnegie's principles are timeless, but the way we deliver them must evolve."

SCAN TO LISTEN

 JOE
HART

Contributors (in order of appearance)

Chris Larsen
Next Level Income
USA
https://www.linkedin.com/in/nextlevelincome/
Finance

Melissa Snover
Nourish3d
UK
https://www.linkedin.com/in/melissa-snover-84276920/
Nutrition

Rene Zamora
Sales Manager Now
USA
https://www.linkedin.com/in/renez/
Sales

Prateek Joshi
Plutoshift
India
https://www.linkedin.com/in/prateek-joshi-91047b19
Technology

Surendra Singh
ViAct
Hong Kong
https://www.linkedin.com/in/surendrasinghrawat/
Construction

Timber Barker
Boom Interactive
USA
https://www.linkedin.com/in/
timber-barker-9660194/
AI

Abhishek Kaushik
We Create Problems
India
https://www.linkedin.com/in/
skabhi/
Technology

Denis O'Shea
Mobile Mentor
New Zealand
https://www.linkedin.com/in/
denisosheamobilementor/
Telecommunications

Darin Dawson
BombBomb
USA
https://www.linkedin.com/in/
darin-dawson-6a62351/
Video

Heidi Dugan
Arete
China
https://www.linkedin.com/
in/heidi-dugan/
Retail

Tim Ringel
Meet the People
USA
https://www.linkedin.com/in/
tim-ringel/
Advertising

Yong-Soo Chung
Urban EveryDay Carry
USA
https://www.linkedin.com/in/
yongsoo/
Consumer Online

Mark Asquith
Captivate
UK
https://www.linkedin.com/in/
markasquith/
Podcasting

Drew Vernon
Tonies®
Germany
https://www.linkedin.com/in/
drewvernon/
Children's Toys

Ed Vincent
Festival Pass
USA
https://www.linkedin.com/in/
edvincent/
Event Management

Ross Veitch
Wego
Singapore
https://www.linkedin.com/in/
rossveitch/
Travel

Chris Schutrups
The Mortgage Hut
Southampton
https://www.linkedin.com/in/
schutrups/
Finance

Eric Schmidt
Glue Up
USA
https://www.linkedin.com/in/
ericschmidtglueup/
Membership Services

Brad Sugars
ActionCOACH
USA, Australia

https://www.linkedin.com/in/
bradsugars/
Coaching

Jonathan Rosenfeld
Rosenfeld Injury Lawyers LLC
USA
https://www.linkedin.com/in/
jonathanrosenfeld/
Legal Services

Mona Akmal
Falkon
USA
https://www.linkedin.com/in/
mona-akmal/
Technology

Aron Clymer
Data Clymer
USA
https://www.linkedin.com/in/
aronclymer/
Technology

Emeric Ernoult
AgoraPulse
France
https://www.linkedin.com/in/
ernoult/
Technology

Gail Kasper
Gail Kasper Enterprises
USA
https://www.linkedin.com/in/
gailkasper/
Coaching

DC Palter
Tech Coast Angels
USA
https://www.linkedin.com/in/
dc-palter/
Authorship

Karen Frame
Makeena
USA
https://linkedin.com/in/
karensframe/
Online Retail

Christian Espinosa
Christian Espinosa, LLC
USA
https://www.linkedin.com/in/
christianespinosa/
Blue Goat Cyber

Bart-Jan Leyts
Loreca
Belgium

https://www.linkedin.com/in/
bart-jan-leyts-b427151b1/
Hospitality

Jason Tan
DDA Labs & Engage AI
Australia
https://www.linkedin.com/
in/jpctan/
AI

Mark Myers
Peak Profit Solutions
USA
https://www.linkedin.com/in/
markshannonmyers/
Taxation

Karen Tan
The Projector
Singapore
https://www.linkedin.com/in/
karen-tan-19980913
Cinema Management

Charles Read
GetPayroll
USA
https://www.linkedin.com/
company/10964861/
Finance

Peter Mann
Oransi
USA
https://www.linkedin.com/in/
peter-mann/
Consumer Appliances

Mathias Boissonot
Handprint
Indonesia
https://www.linkedin.com/in/
boissonot/
Environmental

Jamie Marshall
Everon
UK
http://www.linkedin.com/in/
everonjamiemarshall
IT Services

Jade Gray
Off-Piste Provisions
New Zealand
https://www.linkedin.com/in/
jade-gray-a61b297/
Natural Wholefoods

Terresa Zimmerman
Wood Underwear LLC
USA

https://www.linkedin.com/
company/wood-underwear/
Consumer Fashion

Jill Poet
Organisation for Responsible
Businesses (ORB)
UK
https://www.linkedin.com/
in/jillpoet/
Corporate Governance

Izzy Rosenzweig
Portless
USA
https://www.linkedin.com/in/
izzy-rosenzweig-13653846/
Logistics

Mathieu Johnson
Marble
UK
https://www.linkedin.com/in/
mathieujohnsson/
Conservation

Dre Baldwin
Work On Your Game
USA
http://linkedin.com/in/dreallday
Coaching

Vikas Garg
aBillion
Singapore
https://www.linkedin.com/in/
vikas-garg/
Consumer Lifestyle

Ali Wing
Oobli
USA
https://www.linkedin.com/in/
aliwing/
Food Technology

Mark Wong
IMPOSSIBREW®
UK
https://www.linkedin.com/in/
markwonginfo/
Beverages

Chris Troka
Focused-Biz
USA
https://www.linkedin.com/in/
christopher-troka-3a093058/
Wedding Services

Hussein Hallak
Momentable.art
Egypt

https://www.linkedin.com/in/
husseinhallak/
Art

Roberto Capodieci
SimFly.io
Indonesia
https://linkedin.com/in/rc10
Game Simulator

John Prothro
Foot Solutions
USA
https://www.linkedin.com/
in/johnprothro/
Foot Wellness

Annie Yang
Annie Yang Financial
USA
https://linkedin.com/in/
annieyangfinancial/
Personal Finance

Joe Hart
Dale Carnegie
USA
https://www.linkedin.com/in/
josephkhart
Personal Development

Resources

Guests shared useful books and podcasts with me. I've included them here to make a reading list for you. Do note that some of the guests have their own books. Authorship is part of the way that entrepreneurs share their vision with a broader audience, and establish their authority.

Books

$100M Offers by Alex Hormosi
1001 Ways to Save Money by Annie Yang
Blockchain Revolution by Don Tapscott
Blue Ocean Strategy by W. Chan Kim and Renée Mauborgne
Building a StoryBrand by Donald Miller
Buying Customers by Brad Sugars
Content Inc. by Joe Pulizzi
Contagious: How to Build Word of Mouth in the Digital Age by Jonah Berger
Crushing It! by Gary Vaynerchuk
Crossing the Chasm by Geoffrey A. Moore
Cradle to Cradle: Remaking the Way We Make Things by Michael Braungart and William McDonough
Dropshipping Shopify 2024: The Ultimate Guide to Succeeding in the Lucrative Ecommerce Market by Brad V. Guy

Franchise Your Business by Mark Siebert

From Grass Roots to Greatness. 13 Rules to Build Iconic Brands with Community Led Growth, by Lloyed Lobo

Green to Gold by Daniel C. Esty and Andrew S. Winston

Hooked: How to Build HabitForming Products by Nir Eyal

How to Win Friends and Influence People by Dale Carnegie

Hug Your Customers by Jack Mitchell

Influence: The Psychology of Persuasion by Robert Cialdini

Influence in Action: How to Build Your Conversational Capacity, Do Meaningful Work, and Make a Powerful Difference by Amy Jen Su

Invisible Influence by Jonah Berger

Lean Startup by Eric Ries

LinkedIn Riches by John Nemo

Marketing for IT Services by Jessica McMickens

Marketing 4.0: Moving from Traditional to Digital by Philip Kotler

Masters of Scale by Reid Hoffman

Mindset by Carol S. Dweck

More Than My Share of It All by Kelly Johnson

Netflix, No Rules by Reed Hastings

Niche Down: How to Become Legendary by Being Different by Christopher Lochhead

Purple Cow: Transform Your Business by Being Remarkable by Seth Godin

Published by Chandler Bolt

Raise Your Hand Marketing by Brad Sugars

Range by David Epstein

Rehumanize Your Business by Ethan Beute and Stephen Pacinelli

Scale of Success by Jan Cavelle

Start With Why by Simon Sinek

Start for Success by Jan Cavelle

Supply Chain Management For Dummies by Daniel Stanton
Take Command by Joe Hart
Tech Wise Family by Andy Crouch
The 5-Day Job Search by Annie Yang
The Art of Membership: How to Attract, Retain and Cement Member Loyalty by Sheri Jacobs
The Big Disruption by Jessica Powell
The Culture Map by Erin Meyer
The e-Myth Revisited by Michael Gerber
The End of History and the Last Man by Francis Fukuyama
The In Between by Christian Espinosa
The Payroll Book: A Guide For Small Businesses by Charles Read
The Responsible Company by Yvon Chouinard and Vincent Stanley
The Smartest Person in the Room by Christian Espinosa
The Tipping Point: How Little Things Can Make a Big Difference by Malcolm Gladwell
Tribes by Seth Godin
Work On Your Game by Dre Baldwin
Write. Publish. Repeat. by Sean Platt and Johnny B. Truant
Zero to One by Peter Thiel

Podcasts

Here is the list of podcasts organised alphabetically by title. You'll notice that a few contributors have their own shows.

"Breaking Banks" focuses on innovations in banking and blockchain with Roberto Capodieci
"Build" with Leila Hormozi
"First Class Founders" for hearing directly from Yong-Soo Chung about frameworks and strategies in building a successful business

"Global Business China" provides insights into conducting business in China, covering cultural and regulatory nuances

"HBR IdeaCast" from *Harvard Business Review*

"How I Built This" with Guy Raz

"Infinite Machine Learning" with Prateek Joshi

"Life Coach School" with Brooke Castillo

"Listen Masters, The Shopify Podcast"

"Marketing Over Coffee" with John Wall and Christopher Penn

"Masters of Scale" hosted by Reid Hoffman

"Next Level Income" with Rene Zamora

"Online Marketing Made Easy" by Amy Porterfield

"Social Media Marketing Podcast" with Michael Stelzner

"Social Media ROI" by Olivier Blanchard

"Systematise for Success" with Dr. Steve Day

"Talk Like TED" by Carmine Gallo

"The Big Success Podcast" with Brad Sugars

"The Drone Radio Show" with Randy Goers

"The Logistics Podcast" with Informa

"The Product Startup Podcast" with Kevin Mako

"The Self Publishing Show" with Mark Dawson

"The Speaker Lab" with Grant Baldwin

"All In The Sustainable Business" with Mark Lee, David Grayson, and Chris Coulter

"The Thank You Economy" with Gary Vaynerchuk

"The Tim Ferriss Show"

"The UnNoticed Entrepreneur" with Jim James

"WriteMinded" with Brooke Warner and Grant Faulkner

Tech Stack Apps

There are literally thousands of martech apps to choose from. I've included the apps mentioned by the entrepreneurs in this book.

[Capterra.com is a really useful comparison website].

1. Analytics and Data Management
   Google Sheets
   - URL: [Google Sheets](https://www.google.com/sheets/about)
   - Description: A versatile spreadsheet tool that facilitates simple, collaborative tracking of data, analysis, and automation of tasks.
   SEMrush
   - URL: [SEMrush](https://www.semrush.com)
   - Description: A comprehensive platform for SEO, PPC, and competitive analysis, helping you enhance your online visibility and marketing efforts.
   Handprint
   - URL: [Handprint](https://handprint.tech/calculator)
   - Description: Technology for impact measurement and reporting, focusing on environmental and sustainability metrics.
2. Automation and Workflow Integration
   Zapier
   - URL: [Zapier](https://zapier.com)
   - Description: Zapier automates workflows by connecting your apps and services, enabling you to automate repetitive tasks without coding or relying on developers to build the integration.
   EngageAI
   - URL: [EngageAI](https://www.engageai.com)
   - Description: Direct application for automating engagement on LinkedIn, enhancing your social media interactions and activity through automation.
   Lead Central
   - URL: [Lead Central](https://leadcentral.com)

- Description: Specialises in LinkedIn automation, helping users streamline their lead generation and engagement processes on the platform.

PipeDrive
- URL: [Pipe Drive](https://www.pipedrive.com)
- Description: A sales management tool designed to help small sales teams manage intricate or lengthy sales processes in a more organised and time-efficient manner.

3. Content Creation and Editing

Adobe Premiere Pro
- URL: [Adobe Premiere Pro](https://www.adobe.com/products/premiere.html)
- Description: Industry-standard video editing software used for editing any type of video content with high-level professional tools and capabilities.

Canva
- URL: [Canva](https://www.canva.com)
- Description: An intuitive design tool used for creating graphics, presentations, posters, documents, and other visual content easily and collaboratively.

Descript
- URL: [Descript](https://www.descript.com)
- Description: Offers tools for video and audio editing, enabling easy recording, editing, and producing media, including features like automatic transcription and overdub.

Dreamwave.ai
- URL: [Dreamwave.ai](https://www.dreamwave.ai)
- Description: Provides AI-enhanced tools for photo retouching and creating artistic visual content.

DabbleWriter
- URL: [DabbleWriter](https://www.dabblewriter.com)

- Description: A tool for writers, offering a clean, distraction-free environment for crafting novels, stories, and other written works.

Scrivener
- URL: [Scrivener](https://www.literatureandlatte.com/scrivener/overview)
- Description: A powerful content-generation tool for writers that allows them to structure complex documents, such as scripts, manuscripts, and research papers.

Vimeo
- URL: [Vimeo](https://vimeo.com)
- Description: Known for high-quality video hosting, Vimeo also provides tools for video creation, editing, and broadcasting tailored to professional filmmakers and businesses.

Loom
- URL: [Loom](https://www.loom.com)
- Description: Enables easy recording and sharing of video messages, useful for tutorials, team updates, and more through a simple interface.

4. Customer Relationship Management (CRM)

Salesforce
- URL: [Salesforce](https://www.salesforce.com)
- Description: A comprehensive CRM platform that helps businesses manage customer information, track sales leads, and conduct and monitor marketing campaigns.

HubSpot CRM
- URL: [HubSpot CRM](https://www.hubspot.com/products/crm)
- Description: A robust CRM tool that integrates marketing, sales, and service data to provide a full view of customer interactions and enhance relationship management.

EngageBay
- URL: [EngageBay](https://www.engagebay.com)
- Description: A versatile CRM that integrates marketing efforts with client management to streamline customer interactions and business processes.

PartnerStack
- URL: [PartnerStack](https://partnerstack.com)
- Description: Focuses on managing affiliate, referral, and reseller partnerships, making it easier for businesses to scale through indirect sales channels.

5. E-commerce and Business Management

Shopify
- URL: [Shopify](https://www.shopify.com)
- Description: A leading e-commerce platform that allows businesses to set up an online store and sell their products, offering powerful tools to manage everything from inventory to payments.

Kajabi
- URL: [Kajabi](https://kajabi.com)
- Description: More than just a community platform, Kajabi provides integrated tools for building and managing online courses, marketing automation, and customer engagement, making it ideal for online educators and influencers.

OpenSea
- URL: [OpenSea](https://opensea.io)
- Description: The largest marketplace for buying and selling non-fungible tokens, which are increasingly used by businesses for digital asset management and commerce.

6. Educational and Learning Platforms

Kajabi
- URL: [Kajabi](https://kajabi.com)

- Description: A comprehensive platform for online course creation and management, Kajabi integrates tools for marketing, payments, and student engagement, making it ideal for educators and influencers.

Mighty Networks
- URL: [Mighty Networks](https://www.mightynetworks.com)
- Description: Enables creators to bring together content, community, and commerce in one place, facilitating the creation of courses and managing vibrant learning communities.

7. Email Marketing and Communication

Certainly! Here's the updated list for the Email Marketing and Communication category with the addition of Mailchimp and AWeber, complete with URLs and brief descriptions:

BombBomb
- URL: [BombBomb](https://bombbomb.com)
- Description: Enhances email communication by enabling the sending of video emails, which can be particularly effective for marketing and customer engagement.

Infusionsoft (by Keap)
- URL: [Infusionsoft](https://keap.com/infusionsoft)
- Description: A robust email marketing and sales platform that helps small businesses automate their marketing campaigns and streamline customer interactions.

Mailchimp
- URL: [Mailchimp](https://mailchimp.com)
- Description: A leading all-in-one marketing platform that helps you manage and talk to your clients, customers, and other interested parties. Its approach to marketing focuses on healthy contact management practices, beautifully designed campaigns, and powerful data analysis.

AWeber
- URL: [AWeber](https://www.aweber.com)
- Description: An email marketing service provider with over 20 years of experience helping small businesses automate email follow-up and newsletter delivery for streamlined communication campaigns.

8. **Event Management and Networking**
Meetup
- URL: [Meetup](https://www.meetup.com)
- Description: An excellent platform for organising and finding industry-related events where you can speak or network, facilitating community building and professional networking.

GlueUp
- URL: [GlueUp](https://www.glueup.com)
- Description: A comprehensive platform for managing professional communities and events. GlueUp helps streamline operations for organisations, enhance member engagement, and maximise the impact of networking through its suite of integrated solutions.

9. **Online Chat and Customer Engagement**
Intercom
- URL: [Intercom](www.intercom.com)
- Description: Intercom is a versatile communication platform that helps businesses connect with customers through live chat, chatbots, and more. Known for its user-friendly interface and robust automation capabilities that streamline customer engagement and support.

Drift
- URL: [Drift](www.drift.com)

- Description: Drift is primarily a conversational marketing platform that offers live chat and automated chatbot services. It's designed to help businesses engage customers at every step of the buying process, providing a more personalised experience and boosting conversion rates.

LivePerson
- URL: [LivePerson](www.liveperson.com)
- Description: LivePerson specialises in conversational AI and real-time messaging, offering tools that allow companies to manage customer interactions across various messaging platforms. Geared towards enterprises looking for scalable solutions to enhance customer service and drive sales through AI-driven chats.

Zendesk
- URL: [Zendesk](www.zendesk.com)
- Description: Zendesk is a widely recognised customer service platform that offers a comprehensive suite of tools including a powerful chat feature. It integrates seamlessly with other Zendesk products, providing a full customer support solution that includes ticketing, live chat, an AI-powered knowledge base, and more.

10. Partnership and Affiliate Management

PartnerStack
- URL: [PartnerStack](https://www.partnerstack.com)
- Description: Designed to help companies grow through partnerships, PartnerStack specialises in tools for managing affiliate, referral, and reseller channels effectively.

ReferralCandy
- URL: [ReferralCandy](https://www.referralcandy.com)

- Description: An automated system that allows e-commerce businesses to reward their customers for referrals, enhancing word-of-mouth marketing efforts.

11. Payment and Transaction Systems

    Here are the software tools from your document that fit into the Payment and Transaction Systems category, complete with URLs and brief descriptions:

    Stripe

    - URL: [Stripe](https://stripe.com)
    - Description: A powerful platform for handling online payments, Stripe provides infrastructure for internet businesses to accept payments, manage transactions, and build economic connections globally.

12. Project and Task Management

    Here are the software tools that fit into the Project and Task Management category from your document, complete with URLs and brief descriptions:

    Asana

    - URL: [Asana](https://asana.com)
    - Description: Asana is a project management tool designed to help teams organise, track, and manage their work efficiently, providing features to plan projects, assign tasks, and follow team members' progress.

    Slack

    - URL: [Slack](https://slack.com)
    - Description: Although primarily known for its communication capabilities, Slack also serves as a hub for integrating various project management tools, allowing teams to collaborate and manage tasks directly within the platform.

13. Review and Feedback Platforms
Yelp
- URL: [Yelp](https://www.yelp.com)
- Description: Yelp provides user reviews and recommendations of restaurants, shopping, nightlife, entertainment, services, and more, making it a primary tool for local business reviews.
TripAdvisor
- URL: [TripAdvisor](https://www.tripadvisor.com)
- Description: Specialises in reviews for travel-related content, including hotels, restaurants, and attractions, helping travellers make informed decisions.
Google Reviews
- URL: [Google Reviews](https://www.google.com/maps)
- Description: Integrated with Google Maps, this platform allows users to post and read reviews of businesses, contributing to local SEO and consumer decision-making.
Amazon Customer Reviews
- URL: [Amazon Customer Reviews](https://www.amazon.com)
- Description: Provides feedback on products purchased through Amazon, influencing purchasing decisions with user-generated content.
Trustpilot
- URL: [Trustpilot](https://www.trustpilot.com)
- Description: A global online review community that publishes reviews for businesses worldwide, enhancing brand trust and transparency.
Feefo
- URL: [Feefo](https://www.feefo.com)

- Description: Collects genuine, verified reviews for businesses, focusing on authenticity to boost consumer confidence and business credibility.

14. SEO and Marketing Tools

    Here are the software tools from your document that fit into the SEO and Marketing Tools category, complete with URLs and brief descriptions:

    SEMrush

    - URL: [SEMrush](https://www.semrush.com)
    - Description: A comprehensive tool for SEO, content marketing, competitor analysis, PPC, and social media marketing, designed to help marketers achieve online visibility.

    Ahrefs

    - URL: [Ahrefs](https://ahrefs.com)
    - Description: All-in-one SEO toolset that helps you optimise your website, analyse your competitors, study what your customers are searching for, and track your ranking progress.

    BuzzSumo

    - URL: [BuzzSumo](https://buzzsumo.com)
    - Description: This tool allows you to discover engaging content and outreach opportunities by analysing what content performs best for any topic or competitor.

    Onalytica

    - URL: [Onalytica](https://onalytica.com)
    - Description: Specialises in providing influencer marketing software that helps you identify influential profiles and manage your relationships with them.

15. Social Media and Community Management
Agorapulse
- URL: [Agorapulse](https://www.agorapulse.com)
- Description: A social media management tool that helps businesses streamline their social media interactions across multiple platforms, providing scheduling, monitoring, and reporting features.

Buffer
- URL: [Buffer](https://buffer.com)
- Description: Provides tools for scheduling posts, analysing performance, and managing all your social media accounts in one place to maintain a consistent online presence.

Circle
- URL: [Circle](https://circle.so)
- Description: Offers a flexible and feature-rich platform suited for creators and brands looking to host and manage their online communities, integrating well with other tools.

Discord
- URL: [Discord](https://discord.com)
- Description: Originally popular among gamers, now supports a broad range of community features, including text, voice, and video communications, along with robust moderation and integration capabilities.

Kajabi
- URL: [Kajabi](https://kajabi.com)
- Description: Integrates community building as part of its comprehensive business platform, ideal for online educators and influencers who need tools for course creation, email marketing, and more.

*Tribe
- URL: [Tribe](https://tribe.so)
- Description: A customizable community platform that allows you to create a branded online community to connect, engage, and retain customers, enhancing the user experience with social elements.

16. Video Communications

Zoom
- URL: [Zoom](https://zoom.us)
- Description: Recognised for its reliable video communications, offering features such as video conferencing, webinars, and simple screen recording capabilities.

Microsoft Teams
- URL: [Microsoft Teams](https://teams.microsoft.com)
- Description: A platform that integrates well with Microsoft's suite of products, offering chat, meetings, calls, and collaboration all in one place.

BombBomb
- URL: [BombBomb](https://bombbomb.com)
- Description: Helps you send video emails for more effective communication and engagement, particularly useful for marketing and customer service.

I do have some affiliate links also on my website. From this page, you can click directly to the app page. There are some that aren't mentioned in this list, which may also be useful to you. Affiliates don't cost you any more, but if you buy from the vendor they may give me a modest commission.

https://theunnoticed.cc/affiliates

Ten Take Aways

As an end note, I wanted to try to summarise the recurring themes that I have encountered, not just in these 50 interviews but in over 500 podcast sessions.

This final section attempts to distil those lessons into 10 key themes that are not just business strategies, but reflections of our human need for recognition and validation. Just as individuals seek to be seen and valued, so too do businesses.

Achieving recognition is the ultimate proof of a concept's validity.

Whether it's about staying true to your brand, clearly defining your purpose, or persisting through challenges, these insights are about more than just business – they're about the fundamental human drive to make a meaningful impact.

1. Clarity of Purpose
   - Description: Knowing why you're in business and what you're aiming to achieve is crucial. This clear purpose guides every decision, keeps your team focused, and helps customers understand why they should care about your brand. It's all about having that North Star that everyone can rally around.

2. Authenticity
   - Description: Be true to what your brand promises. If you say you're all about customer service, then go above and beyond for your customers. Live your brand's values every day. When the founder embodies the brand's promise, it sets a powerful example for the entire team.
3. Identify Strategic Early Adopters
   - Description: Find and engage with those first few customers who are excited about new things and willing to give your product a shot. These folks are often trendsetters, and their early support can help build momentum.
4. Promote Insight-Driven Revenue Generation
   - Description: Combine the power of your marketing, sales, and customer success teams by using data to make smarter decisions. When everyone's on the same page and working from the same playbook, it's easier to spot opportunities and boost your bottom line.
5. Engage Thought Leadership for Market Education
   - Description: Share your expertise through blogs, podcasts, and speaking gigs. Helping your audience understand the tough issues positions you as a go-to expert and builds trust.
6. Build a Targeted Influencer Network
   - Description: Work with influencers who resonate with your brand and have a following in your target market. Their endorsement can amplify your message and build credibility.
7. Optimise Omnichannel Engagement Strategies
   - Description: Be where your customers are. Whether it's LinkedIn for B2B or TikTok for a younger crowd, use the right platforms to share engaging content that resonates with them.

8. Utilise Simplified, Common Tools for Goals Alignment
   - Description: Use easy-to-access tools like Google spreadsheets to keep track of your goals. This way, everyone knows what's important and can see how their work fits into the bigger picture.
9. Develop a Distinct Brand Identity
   - Description: Make sure your brand stands out and that everything you put out there reflects who you are. Consistency in your message and visuals helps people recognise and remember you.
10. Perseverance
    - Description: Every entrepreneur faces setbacks, but the key is to keep pushing forward. Get up every day as if it's a new day, learn from your failures, and keep moving. Perseverance is about staying resilient and focused on your goals, no matter the obstacles.

More Take Aways.

I've created a longer document, which includes key take aways from each interview. If you would like a free download of this, then just go to this website page:

https://www.jimajames.com/unnoticed-vol-three

About the Author

I jumped from a plane at 17 and have never looked back, or down, ever since. That experience, 2,000 feet over the glorious fields of Kent on a spring morning in 1989, taught me the power of a well-publicized idea to generate profits.

For over 25 years, I lived as an expatriate entrepreneur in Singapore and China, founding and leading ventures in public relations, internet marketing, car imports, energy drink distribution, and recruitment services. I have been involved in nonprofits, including co-founding the Beijing Chapter of EO, starting the British Business Awards in China, and being on the boards of the British Chambers in Singapore and China. I also served as the interim CEO of Lotus Cars in China.

In addition to my businesses, I've received British Chamber SME of the Year in Singapore and Beijing's Top Touch Awards "International Innovator of the Year."

Of course, I have had my share of failures, too. It is often when plans don't work out that I've learnt the most about myself and tested my limits of passion, mental strength, and persistence in the face of what, at times, seemed overwhelming odds. But that's the life of an entrepreneur. We trade comfort for excitement, security for passion, and live with the excitement of creating value out of thin air.... just like I did with that parachute jump.

These experiences have made me appreciate the importance of a good network of peers, my health, and taking time to enjoy the journey.

After Asia, I returned to the UK with Erika, my Shanghainese wife, our daughters Amity Huan Huan and Halo Mulan, our Beijing Beagle Binkie, and our rescue cat Samuel J.

I've lived a life primarily on my own terms by getting customers to buy into the brands I have built. Not everyone knows how to do that. Seeing founders more worthy than me of recognition for what they do made me decide to make it my mission to help the unnoticed entrepreneur.

I do this by sharing the experiences of business owners on my podcast, in these books, via my courses, and consultancy.

Please get in touch and get noticed:

https://www.jimajames.com

Index

N

Naturally Bolder, 157
Nature, technology (combination),
258–259
Needs, customised solutions, 170
Netflix, impact, 277
Networking
discrete networking, 239
importance, 170
opportunities, capitalisation, 52
power, 67
Networks, leveraging, 151
Next Level Income, genesis, 6
Ng, Gary, 24
Niche, 281
audience, finding/targeting,
150, 163
finding, 180–181
marketing, 86
Niching
insights, 284
power, 282
Niching, importance, 210
Nokia, partnership pitch, 42–43
Non-fungible tokens (NFTs), 276
leveraging, 102
power, 102
reaction, 282
rewards, 101
technology, 278
Non-governmental
organization (NGO)
business accountability, 229–230
mobile application, Handprint.
Tech offering, 205
network, leveraging, 204–205

Nourish3d
ambassador programme, 14
genesis, 12
product safety/efficacy,
ensuring, 13
Novel, marketing (challenge), 150
NVIDIA machine learning team, 90

O

Objectives and Key Results (OKRs),
usage, 128
Off-Piste Provisions
business, building, 217
challenges, navigation, 217
community, building, 218
distribution, 218
funds, raising, 219
genesis, 216–217
marketing strategies, packaging/
targeting, 217–218
relationships, maintenance, 219
Omnichannel engagement strategies,
optimisation, 328
One Tree Planted, Wood Underwear
(partnership), 224
Online sampling, leverag-
ing, 259–260
Oobli, 258
marketing strategies, trial/
education, 259–260
mistakes, learning, 260–261
product craveability, 259
Opportunities, 209
Oransi, 198–201
mistakes, learning, 200
products, private labelling, 199

X

Xiaomi, partnership, 80

Y

Yang, Annie Margarita, 292–295
YouTube, usage, 193

Z

Zamora, Rene, 18–22
Zapier, usage, 61
Zimmerman, Terresa,
    222–224
Zoom (video conferencing tool), 97